"My grandmother quoted the old proverb: To those who have been given a lot, much is expected. That was something I was aware of growing up."

—Patrick Kennedy

"We were all, every one of us, raised to be president."

—Christopher Lawford

"I come from a public family. I work in a public profession, my husband's in a public profession, and I am therefore public, too. But that doesn't mean everything in my life is public."

—Maria Shriver Schwarzenegger

"People are always judging me as my father's son. Someone always seems to notice me. Someone is always scrutinizing me."

—Robert F. Kennedy, Jr.

"Being a Kennedy raises expectations. It is also a source of great pride."

—Kathleen Kennedy Townsend

KENNEDYS

THE NEXT GENERATION

JONATHAN SLEVIN and

MAUREEN SPAGNOLO

ST. MARTIN'S PAPERBACKS

Published by arrangement with National Press, Inc.

KENNEDYS: THE NEXT GENERATION

Copyright © 1990 by National Press Books, Inc.
Update copyright © 1992 by National Press Books, Inc.

Cover photograph credits: Caroline Schlossberg, courtesy Ron Galella, Ltd. Maria Shriver, Smed/Galella Ltd. Willie Smith, courtesy Ron Galella, Ltd. John Kennedy Jr., Bettmann Archive.

Library of Congress Catalog Card Number: 89-12604

ISBN: 0-312-92860-2

Printed in the United States of America

National Press Books hardcover edition published 1990
St. Martin's Paperbacks edition/October 1992

10 9 8 7 6 5 4 3 2 1

Acknowledgments

We are grateful for the participation of Kennedy family members Patrick, Kathleen, Robert Jr., Michael, Rory; Bobby, Maria and Timothy Shriver and numerous friends, including Chris and Erin Nocera, Angie Novello, John Seigenthaler, Melody Miller, Dave Powers, Jim Vallee, Jean Fleischman and Maggie O'Neill. We would like to thank the staffs of the John F. Kennedy Library and the Joseph P. Kennedy Jr. Foundation for their assistance. Special thanks must be given to the Kennedy Library for use of the splendid photographic works of the late Frank Teti.

Recognition is due David Ehrlich for his meticulous copy editing.

Contents

Rose Fitzgerald and Joseph Patrick Kennedy had nine children. Six of them became parents to the twenty-nine members of the next generation who are the subject of this book.

Chapter One: The Children of Jacqueline Bouvier and John Fitzgerald Kennedy   1

John F. Kennedy (1917–1963) was the thirty-fifth president of the United States (1961–63) and was assassinated while in office. His wife was Jacqueline Bouvier, the daughter of a well-connected family in Philadelphia and Newport, Rhode Island. Following her husband's untimely death, Jacqueline remarried, to Aristotle Onassis, a Greek shipping magnate.

Chapter Two: The Children of Eunice Kennedy and Sargent Shriver   29

Eunice Shriver (1921–) married R. Sargent Shriver, an attorney, the first director of the Peace Corps and an unsuccessful vice-presidential candidate in 1972. She and her husband founded the Special Olympics in 1968.

Chapter Three: The Children of Patricia Kennedy and Peter Lawford

Patricia Lawford (1921–) is best known for having started the Very Special Arts (VSA) program, one in which many of the Kennedy children have been involved. Her marriage to actor Peter Lawford ended in divorce in 1965. She has not remarried.

Chapter Four: The Children of Ethel Skakel and Robert Kennedy

Robert F. Kennedy (1925–1968) served as U.S. Attorney General during the administration of his brother and was elected U.S. Senator from New York in 1964. He was a candidate for president in 1968 until he was assassinated. His wife is the former Ethel Skakel, whose roots were in the Chicago area. Ethel has not remarried.

Chapter Five: The Children of Jean Kennedy and Stephen Smith

Jean Smith (1928–) married financier Stephen Smith, who was for many years a close family adviser. Smith died in 1990. Jean initiated a summer day camp program for people with mental retardation at the Smiths' upstate New York retreat.

Chapter Six: The Children of Joan Bennett and Edward Kennedy

Edward M. Kennedy (1932–) has been U.S. Senator from Massachusetts since 1962. He ran unsuccessfully for president in 1980. He was divorced from his wife, Joan Bennett, in 1981.

Contents

Introduction

A day after his election victory, John F. Kennedy was asked what he might like to do after two terms as president. After all, fifty-three is a pretty young age to retire as an elder statesman. With a twinkle in his eye, the president-elect replied, "I'm going to be a rich bum!"

Tragically, John Kennedy and the American people were denied the opportunity of learning what contribution the youngest man ever to be elected president might *really* have made with the rest of his life. Neither he nor his younger brother, Bobby, who might also have been president, lived to be fifty years old. Although Ted, the third brother to reach for the brass ring, fell short of his goal, the notion of three members of the same family coming so close to holding the most powerful office in the world is unprecedented in American history.

Kennedys are perhaps the nearest thing to royalty we have in this country. Not only have they fashioned a dynasty, but they have woven their personal aspirations into the political fabric of the nation. Ambassador Joseph Kennedy, the progenitor of the dynasty, once commented with pride, that Kennedys constituted "the most exclusive club in the world."

A new generation has come of age. Will the twenty-eight living children of Jack, Bobby, Ted and their sisters Eunice, Patricia and Jean carry on the political—and even presidential—tradition established by their forebears?

In the 1970s and 80s, their well-publicized adolescent antics suggested that the next generation might inherit the Kennedy trappings of wealth and prestige but shun the Kennedy values of selflessness and public-mindedness. They appeared headed for a life as rich *and* spoiled bums, acting out the fantasy of JFK without exemplifying his legacy. The extent to which members of the current generation of Kennedys has taken up and will continue to carry the twin family torches of political power and public service is what this study is about.

* * *

While rummaging through family memorabilia at the Kennedy compound in Hyannis Port, Senator Ted Kennedy was asked by a family acquaintance, "Ted, what really happened at Chappaquiddick?" The youngest brother replied, without looking up, "I panicked . . . and blew the presidency."

Ted's presidential campaign in 1980 brought the next generation of Kennedys into contact with an interested, adoring, yet also unforgiving American public. Encounters with the power of the family legacy uplifted the youthful campaigners, just as expressions of concern about the moral character of the current torch-bearer distressed them. For the third generation, Ted's campaign was an initiation rite, yet his loss to Jimmy Carter seared the bitterness of defeat into their consciousness.

Out of that defeat came liberation for some. The American people had set a limit to Ted's robust political career—the U.S. Senate was as far as he could go. The political end of one generation of Kennedys opened the way for the emergence of the next. Assassins had buried Jack and Bobby in the sixties. Ted's own failings led to his demise as a presidential prospect in 1980.

Each Kennedy has dealt differently with that campaign experience—and with how to live life as a Kennedy. Rhode Island State Representative Patrick Kennedy has comfortably created a role in his family legacy. The youngest child of Joan and Ted, and the youngest Kennedy ever to hold elective office, explained what it means for him to be a third generation Kennedy:

> You either act on it or react to it. It's an either/or decision. You either like it and move in that direction or if you don't, it's because you don't like it and you're going to run away from it and do something very different. In either case it's going to shape what you are.

By contrast, Ethel and Bobby's oldest son is reacting to his heritage as much as acknowledging it. U.S. Representative Joseph Kennedy II announced, "I hate the word 'legacy.' There's a tremendous inclination out there to think that somehow I feel some crazy obligation to pick up—what would it be—the 'torch?' "

In the sixties, JFK, in the words of his nephew Steve Smith Jr., gave the nation a sense of its "collective possibility." RFK grew to personify the nation's moral conscience. But in the seventies, Ted carried a flickering torch through a period of national struggle and perceived decline. Ted's legislative activism and the growth of the Special Olympics placed a less distinct—though still honorable—stamp on the eighties. In the nineties, confronting a nation striving for rediscovery and renewal, what might the next generation of Kennedys contribute? While some of this generation are linking the cause of the American people to their personal destiny, others have shied away from the demands of a public life.

The Kennedy family "book of manners" does not require members to hold political office. However, it does hold it improper to live an unexceptional life. Some can be—and some members of the next generation are—teachers, administrators, journalists, social activists, capitalists, actors and lawyers. They are required only to do well, and they must not forget the old Kennedy credo to do unto others . . . and to help the handicapped and the poor.

* * *

A study of the next generation of Kennedys would be incomplete without explaining the Associate Trustees system, formalized in 1987 by the trustees of the Joseph P. Kennedy Jr. Foundation to help support charitable projects of the third generation.

Although far smaller than the Rockefeller or Ford Foundations, the Kennedy Foundation has targeted $2.5 million for projects developed by the patriarch's grandchildren for each of the past three years. Members of the third generation are encouraged to begin any charity they desire, as long as it in some way benefits persons with mental retardation. John Jr. recently made the news with his new charity: a program to help educate and train those who work with the mentally and developmentally disabled.

The cousins offer their name and some of their time, while a skilled staff provides support and expertise. Foundation funds are earmarked for startup costs only, in amounts such as the $100,000 awarded to John's project. After a year or so funding from other sources must be found.

To date, twelve of the Kennedy grandchildren are involved in such projects. Some they originated; others they helped to expand. One of the most successful programs is Best Buddies, a nationwide support system involving college students and people with disabilities, started by Anthony Shriver while a student at Georgetown University.

Kennedys are willing to talk about the philanthropic Associate Trustees program. By contrast, a shroud of reticence covers the family's Park Agency company, which manages the family's business interests and financial affairs. The next generation benefits directly from the low-profile New York-based enterprise, which Stephen Smith ran until his death in August 1990. The staff provides the cousins with many perks and services, such as a travel agency, accounting, and loans to finance political campaigns.

* * *

Like their parents and grandparents before them, members of the next generation have learned to deal with the press. They have mastered the art of controlling their emotions in public and dispensing—or withholding —access and information. Although some profess the desire to live what they call a "normal" life, they all share the responsibility to uphold their family legacy and thereby sustain the mystique.

The next generation responded in different ways to the writing and compiling of this book. The editors anticipated cooperation from those in politics and public positions: Kathleen, Joe, Kerry, Michael, Maria Shriver, Teddy Jr. and Patrick.

Bobby Kennedy Jr., one of the Kennedys who has been very active behind the scenes, agreed to an interview with writer Tom Andersen.

Bobby Shriver never intended to give much of an interview, or to talk about himself. "I've done nothing special. I prefer not to be written about," he told our writer. Ninety minutes later Bobby exclaimed, "I can't believe I've been talking to you for this long. I said yesterday I wasn't going to do this and now you've wound up with an exclusive!"

John and Caroline maintained their policy of refusing interviews, asking politely to be allowed to live their lives in peace. John seeks nothing from others except the privilege of normal expectations.

In compiling this book, we decided that not all the Kennedy cousins were of equal interest to the public. A number of them—Timothy, Mark and Anthony Shriver; and Stephen and William Smith—have chosen professional paths that lead to more private lives. Others—Chris, Douglas and Rory Kennedy; and Amanda and Kym Smith—are too young to have chosen a direction for themselves. Therefore, the profiles on these individuals are brief. We focused on the older and more public cousins, such as Kathleen, Joe, Michael and Kerry Kennedy; and Maria Shriver. There are exceptions—Caroline and John Kennedy are included because of their celebrity status; David and Teddy Jr., because their lives have affected all the others; and Patrick, although in the younger group, has already stepped into the public arena.

Kennedys are willing to use the power of the press to promote themselves and their various causes and interests, as long as they can direct what information goes out, and when. In fact, the essence of Kennedy power derives a great deal from understanding and using the art of public communication, a lesson taught well by Grandfather Joseph (*It's not what you are that counts*).

Kennedy power goes beyond what can be attained through wealth. It is an intangible substance, freely given by the people in a democratic society, and thus all the more appealing. When Kennedys gather together twenty or so years down the road to set their sights on the White House again, the Hyannis Port hearth may no longer be large enough for a clan that now also includes Schwarzeneggers, Cuomos, Schlossbergs, Townsends, Allens and McKelveys. It is hardly prophecy to expect a future run for president. Here they are in their formative years: a family of artists whose medium is power.

Jonathan Slevin and Maureen Spagnolo

KENNEDYS

THE NEXT GENERATION

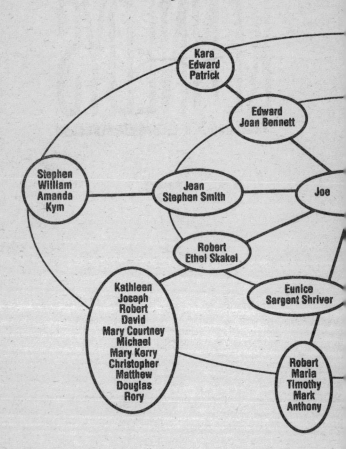

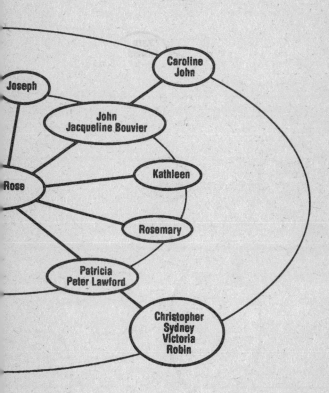

N N E D Y S

Caroline
John

Joseph

John
Jacqueline Bouvier

Kathleen

Rose

Rosemary

Patricia
Peter Lawford

Christopher
Sydney
Victoria
Robin

CHAPTER ONE

THE CHILDREN OF JACQUELINE BOUVIER AND JOHN FITZGERALD KENNEDY

John F. Kennedy (1917–1963), thirty-fifth president of the United States (1961–1963), established a "New Frontier" and was assassinated while in office. His wife was Jacqueline Bouvier, the daughter of a prominent family in Philadelphia and Newport, Rhode Island. Following her husband's untimely death, Jacqueline remarried, to Aristotle Onassis, a Greek shipping magnate.

Caroline (1957–)
John (1960–)

Caroline Kennedy
A Very Private Person

She is thirty-three years old. She lives with her husband and two daughters in a co-op apartment on Park Avenue. She shops at the local market for her own food. She works out at the Trainer's Edge on Third Avenue and browses at the children's store, Ben's For Kids. Most mornings, her 45-year-old husband walks sixty blocks to work. They have a live-in nanny but the mother—though she has a law degree—has put her career on hold and spends a great deal of time with her children. The family frequents Central Park on weekends.

This could be a description of many well-off New York City women today, except this mother attends society designer Carolina Herrera's fashion shows, shops for baby clothes at the ultrachic Cerutti on Madison Avenue, includes as her friends singer Carly Simon, *Saturday Night Live* producer Lorne Michaels, director Mike Nichols and Alexandra Styron, daughter of novelist William Styron. And one day a week, she sends the children to the Fifth Avenue apartment of grandma—Jacqueline Kennedy Onassis.

It isn't easy being Caroline Kennedy Schlossberg. No matter what she does or who she becomes, America will not forget the small girl who, nearly 30 years ago, ran to her father with glee when he called.

In the twenty-six years since the death of John F. Kennedy, the country has watched Caroline grow up through the lenses of roving photographers. We saw her melancholy face when her mother married Aristotle Onassis. We saw an overweight adolescent who tried to duck the press with downcast eyes and who seemed not to have inherited her mother's exotic beauty. And we were glued to the pictures of her wedding day in 1986, when suddenly—as if a fairy godmother had waved a magic wand—a rail-thin, confident, beautiful young woman emerged from Our Lady of Victory Church in Centerville, Massachusetts, on the arm of her knight in shining armor.

Even so, Caroline has been called "the private Kennedy." Said one acquaintance: "Caroline has had to struggle to get to a place where she can live like a normal person. And she's done it." Considering that the wayside is littered with the carcasses of celebrity offspring, this normality may turn out to be Caroline's greatest achievement. How *did* she do it? Certainly with the help of her mother's unflagging determination to see that her children grew up to be unspoiled, responsible adults.

Yes, that's true, her friends say, but don't overlook the biggest factor in Caroline's life—her seemingly unlikely interfaith marriage to an intellectual thirteen years her senior.

Edwin Schlossberg, the son of a wealthy Jewish textile manufacturer, is president of his own design firm and has often been called a Renaissance man. He holds a Ph.D. in science and literature from Columbia University, has written nine obscure books, and paints, writes poetry, and works at philosophy, inventing, and teaching.

The truth is that Caroline's choice of a husband is actually not so surprising. Friends say that Edwin, whom Caroline met at a dinner party in 1981, has the quality of intelligence and humanism which she likes most in members of her own family. And in him, one friend says, "She has found a warm, witty, down-to-earth, sensitive man—Ed's her protector."

Despite the couple's shared preference for a quiet life-style, the wedding of John F. Kennedy's only daughter was unavoidably an *Event*. As a thousand spectators screamed outside the church and four hundred photographers fought for that golden shot, Caroline's uncle, Ted Kennedy, walked her down the aisle. In the excitement afterward, Edwin's mother took a tumble on the church steps—but that didn't stop her from dancing at a reception where Carly Simon sang *Chapel of Love*.

And in true Kennedy fashion, there were speeches. "We've all thought of Jack today," said her only surviving Kennedy uncle, "and how much he loved Caroline and Jackie." The most moving moment came when John F. Kennedy Jr. rose to toast his sister. "It's been the three of us alone for so long—Mommy, me, and Caroline—and now we've got a fourth." With that, it wasn't only the bride who cried.

Like many women of the 1980s, Caroline wanted to get her career in order before having a baby, so she waited to get pregnant until her last year of law school. Her classmates marveled at her stamina: she didn't miss a single day of school, showing up despite snow and subzero New York winter weather. In May of 1988, Caroline graduated with honors. A month later, on June 25, Rose Kennedy Schlossberg was born.

If Caroline was modern in planning the timing of little Rose's birth, she couldn't be more traditional now that she's a mother. Unlike many of her peers who stay home for a few months and then go back to work, leaving the baby in the charge of a full-time caregiver, Caroline (who, admittedly, can afford to do so) has delayed taking a job in a law firm until Rose is older. She works from home on a project that will, for many, recall her father's Pulitzer-Prize-winning *Profiles in Courage*—a book for William Morrow publishers on the Bill of Rights. However, with the birth of their second daughter, Tatiani, in March 1990, William Morrow may have a bit of a longer wait.

In a somewhat sheltered life, currently confined to

work and family, Caroline has broken away from some family traditions. Last summer, the couple passed up weekends at the Kennedy compound in Hyannis Port or with Jackie at Martha's Vineyard. Instead, they summered in the Hamptons, the community on Long Island's South Fork that is favored by the literary and the artistic.

They have opted for a home-decorating style that is definitely not shared by the society interior designers her mother favors. Instead, their apartment is filled with objects Edwin has collected and furniture he's designed. (Edwin also designed Rose's nursery—a foam-covered chamber full of playthings and wall hangings.)

Still, Caroline has a deep sense of family and legacy. Her decision to name her first daughter after her own grandmother, 100-year-old Rose Kennedy, is indicative of this. Caroline is on the board of the John F. Kennedy Library and is active in the Kennedy Foundation. She also spent two years overseeing the commissioning and design of a memorial to her father that now stands in front of the gold-domed State House in Boston.

Caroline is equally committed to her friends, most of whom date back to her prep-school and college days. As one noted, "Because of who she is, she's much more comfortable and trusting with people she's known a long time. She's *very* careful about letting new people into her life." Another underscored that view: "She's painfully shy, but—like her mother, who loves to dance and swap jokes with friends—Caroline has many moments of ebullience in private."

Caroline's willingness to be her mother's daughter is striking in a generation of Kennedys who as adolescents sowed some wild oats. Other Kennedys have had their problems, yet both Caroline and her brother, John, reached maturity without courting disaster. "Of all the Kennedys," says an acquaintance, "Caroline is the most together and likable."

This is more remarkable considering how difficult it could be to be Jackie's daughter. As a friend of Jackie's said, "All girls have problems with their mothers. But imagine being the daughter of a skinny, beautiful, world object—even at sixty, Jackie is one of the most desirable women in the world."

In fact, as many of Caroline's friends point out, she and Jackie enjoy an extremely close relationship— closer, it's said, than the one Jackie has with her son. "John is determined to have his own life and make his own way," an old family friend commented. "He's so passionate about that idea that he's somewhat removed and private. Jackie doesn't exactly have to trick him to get him up to the apartment, but she has to think of excuses to get him there."

Caroline, on the other hand, is more dutiful and ac-cepting, seeing her mother a couple of times a week. And Jackie is absolutely taken with her granddaughters, with good reason. Two-year-old Rose has the same wide mouth, round face, and saucer eyes that Jackie had at the same age. Jackie seems careful not to spoil Rose, fully aware that the same upbringing that worked so well for her children needs to be given also to the next generation.

This is a parenting philosophy that is shared by Caro-line and Edwin. It doesn't matter to them that Caroline is expected to inherit a hefty chunk of a fortune esti-mated in the hundreds of millions—and that Rose and Tatiani will be a very privileged girls. "Caroline has an enormous amount of integrity," said a friend, "and one of the nicest things about her and Ed is that they respect their wealth and don't flaunt it."

It is probably too much to say that the Kennedy torch has been passed to a new generation; Caroline Kennedy Schlossberg is too private a person to make a cause of her name. But in her sensible and quiet way, she is as much a symbol for her time as her father was for his.

Caroline has made her life choices carefully. She believes implicitly that private satisfactions are just as rewarding as public recognition. As she and her husband watch Rose and Tatiani grow, they are more sure than ever of that conviction. Caroline's ideal world is a very different Camelot—and the best and only way to reach it is to work at it, day by day.

John F. Kennedy Jr.

Disgustingly Normal

It was madness, even by Bloomingdale's standards. The crowd that late-November lunchtime was possessed by an urgency that transcended mere pre-Christmas shopping lust. Suddenly, TV lights burst on. The day's hottest item, John Fitzgerald Kennedy Jr., the son of America's thirty-fifth president, stepped onto a platform, looking amazed and none too happy. Women screamed and cameras started snapping like piranhas.

"Oh dear," he said as he joined cousins Ted Jr., and Willie Smith, Willie's mother, Jean Kennedy Smith, and Lauren Bacall on the store's loge level. "It was mass hysteria," one Bloomingdale's staffer said. "Poor man. I don't think he had any idea."

Very Special Arts (VSA), a Kennedy charity, was behind the event, a sale of boxed Christmas ornaments produced by the retarded in Third World countries. But the TV crews, the screaming women, and the pushing paparazzi didn't care about the cause. They didn't care about Lauren Bacall, either, or the other Kennedy cousins—all associate trustees of the Joseph P. Kennedy Foundation, which had funded the program. They wanted John.

Kennedy took the microphone. "I hope you'll all buy a few boxes," he said. "I'm here to sell boxes, and that's what I want to get to do." Of course, by doing that—or, more precisely, by autographing boxes for a few minutes —he got the ornaments mentioned on seven local news shows and "Entertainment Tonight." Jill Rapaport, a perky Channel 2 News reporter, even got a brief interview.

9

"It's really the boxes they should be coming for, not us," Kennedy told her. But then Rapaport boxed him in, asking how it felt to be one of the world's more eligible bachelors. "C'mon," Kennedy pleaded, eyes and hands turning upward. "I dunno." He glanced away from the microphone hopelessly. Finally, visibly embarrassed, he said, "It feels okay." Cut to Rapaport happy-talking in the studio later. "Kinda cute, huh?" she said to the camera.

Although Bloomingdale's sold almost $50,000 worth of ornaments that day, John Kennedy, 30, considered the appearance disappointing. "We didn't want it to turn out the way it did," says Kathy Walther, a VSA executive. "It was very obnoxious from the second he walked in. John hoped it would be more substantive."

Unfortunately, substance isn't the first thing that comes to most people's minds, when they think of JFK Jr. The first thought, of course, is of the little boy in the blue coat and short pants saluting his father's bronze coffin.

That memory alternates with less high-toned images: Kennedy pumped up and shirtless as *People* magazine's "Sexiest Man Alive." Kennedy linked in the columns with an enviable bevy of beauties—Brooke Shields, Madonna, Daryl Hannah, Molly Ringwald and Princess Stephanie of Monaco.

Those images melded at his political coming-out party—the 1988 Democratic Convention—where John F. Kennedy Jr., tabloid celebrity, was transformed into the living embodiment of a nation's not-quite-impossible dream: that it will wake up one morning to find another JFK in the White House. Uncle Ted passed the torch himself when he had John introduce him to the delegates, and though young John's speech didn't rattle the rafters, there was a surge of emotion in the hall. This was the first time John has ever acted the part of "a Kennedy" on a national stage. And the moment suggested that he could become the ultimate postmodern politician—a blank canvas for fantasies of national destiny.

"Seeking Anonymity"

The boy in the blue coat is grown up now, and whether he likes it or not, people still have their eyes on him. He doesn't like it at all. Friends insist that his life's quest is for anonymity and normality. He may never find privacy ("He's never known life any different," says one friend), but he's won the battle to be normal. Aggressively normal. "Disgustingly normal," according to a pal. "Extraordinarily ordinary."

He is also understandably reluctant to give anything away, having already given so much. Kennedy is "trying to have an open life," said Faith Stevelman, who met him on their second day at NYU Law School, in 1986. "He sure turned out to be completely different than I expected. The press makes him out to be a narcissistic celebrity brat, but he's not. People want to see him that way, because of his father, because of his name, because he's handsome, but—praise to him—he has a life that's much more real than that. He likes being in the world." He doesn't like publicity, though. "It curtails his freedom," Stevelman said.

So aside from lending his name to good causes, he's done nothing to attract attention to himself. He's given only one print interview in his life, to the *New York Times,* and it wasn't particularly revealing. Avoiding reporters "has always been a habit," says his aunt Lee Radziwill. "We're not going to start now."

One former family intimate described the Kennedy family's attitude as "a conspiracy of silence, mandated from above. But when they want to get the message out, they do." John declined to be interviewed for this book. But there's a message his friends want to get out, so many of them cooperated, as did former co-workers and bosses and a few Kennedy family members.

They are setting the stage for what a Kennedy Foundation executive describes as "John emerging into the public sphere." After working for the city of New York, a nonprofit developer, the Reagan Justice Department, and a politically connected Los Angeles law firm, the man who is perhaps the most famous presidential child of the century is now one of about 400 assistant district attorneys in the office of Manhattan prosecutor Robert Morgenthau.

He got the $30,000-a-year job, which friends say he coveted, late last year, after a series of interviews. However, in order to keep it, John must pass the New York bar exam. He has recently taken it for the third time, with results not yet released. According to Joe Marino, his tutor, the odds are in John's favor. Flunkees who take Marino's six-week, $1,075 course have an 80 percent success rate.

Meanwhile, although John's troubles with the exam have drawn snickers from the public—"The Hunk Flunked," the tabloids announced, he is not the first in his family—or in public office—to fail the exam. Robert Jr. failed his first attempt and withdrew from his second test, months before his arrest for heroin possession. He passed the third time. But in contrast, his sister Caroline Schlossberg and cousins Kathleen Kennedy Townsend and Kerry Kennedy Cuomo passed the first time.

Like a favored candidate's spin doctors before a big debate, his friends are trying to lower expectations. Public appearances to the contrary, they seem convinced, and want to convince others, that John Fitzgerald Kennedy Jr.—JFK II—doesn't really exist. "He wants to be perceived as his own man," said Peter Allen, an acquaintance from grade school. And Stevelman added heatedly, "He's not John F. Kennedy Jr. He is himself. It's 'Hi, I'm John.'"

John doesn't exploit the family name, like some of the other Kennedy cousins of his generation. A friend observed: "They might as well have the name emblazoned on their sleeves." John does share many traits with his father, though—and people want to believe he shares even more. Just like his father, he is bound up with his immediate family. "All of our lives, there's just been the three of us—Mommy, Caroline, and I," John said at his sister's wedding. The next circle is a coterie of intensely loyal friends—some of whom go back through prep school. At Brown University, where John earned a bachelor's degree in history in 1983, his friends literally surrounded him, shielding him from the 14,500 spectators during his mile-long graduation processional.

Serious Sex Appeal

John has also inherited his father's charisma. "Even if he wasn't John Kennedy," says his cousin Cecil Auchincloss, "people would notice him at a party—even as a kid." Though he seems to disdain Kennedy competitiveness (when he was a child, the cousins called him "Mama's boy"), John shares his father's love of athletics. An active outdoorsman, he skis, rafts, snorkels, hikes and camps out. "He's an overenergetic, can't-sit-still type," a friend reported.

Also like his father (and like his mother's father, "Black Jack" Bouvier, who had an affair on his honeymoon), John's got serious sex appeal. "The apple doesn't fall far from the tree," said a young woman who knows him. "Girls come and go."

Madonna, this generation's self-styled Marilyn Monroe, set her sights on John. "He and Madonna were good friends," said a fast-crowd friend of the Kennedy cousins. "She was obviously the aggressor."

Friends of John also believe that Madonna initiated all their liaisons. "I think they met when Bobby Shriver made his Special Olympics album," says one pal. "Then

Madonna invited John to her concert at Madison Square Garden. She also works out with the same trainer. I don't think that's chance." Though some insist that John has had "dates" with Madonna between the rounds of her marital bout with Sean Penn, a close friend of the singer's sighed, "If only," when asked if the duo's rumored relationship was real.

Many of John's purported assignations turn out to be fictions. Another Kennedy "date," identified in some papers as Molly Ringwald, was actually John's steady girlfriend of four years, actress Christina Haag. "A good thing," a friend jokes. "Christina would have believed it."

Haag, the daughter of a retired businessman, grew up in Manhattan. She is not the blueblood she's sometimes made out to be; she's an actress struggling to make ends meet. A graduate of the Juilliard School of Music, she has played Ophelia at Center Stage in Baltimore, acted in *A Matter of Degrees,* an independent film about college students, and played a hospital public relations officer in *The Littlest Victim,* a TV movie about a doctor who treats children with AIDS. Between jobs, she has checked coats at Elio's, a New York power restaurant, and worked as an assistant to Seventh Avenue designer Christine Thomson.

Luckily, both John and Christine know Daryl Hannah and knew it wasn't true when, in late 1989, Suzy's column in the *New York Post* reported that he'd proposed to the star. Said a Kennedy friend, "They've all known each other for years." A gossip item once appeared saying that Hannah, the daughter of a Chicago real-estate magnate, had followed college-age John down the beach on St. Martin. "They were twelve at the time," laughed the friend, "and I bet he followed her. If she'd been following him, he would have stopped."

Then there are the models. Kennedy has met some through Richard Wiese, a Phi Psi fraternity brother at

Brown who is now a Ford model. Audra Avizienia, a model, told *People* she had dated John. Now she claims the magazine misquoted her. *People*'s reporter denies it. So has she gone out with him? "That's beside the point," Avizienia snapped.

An older friend of the family considers all this par for the course. "Kennedys love beautiful people—winners. They like movie stars like everyone else. But everyone else isn't moving in those circles all the time. Kennedy men are intensely, highly sexed. There's a lot of activity. But the women they marry are solid gold. They need both and they get it. Why not have the cream of the crop?"

Pranks and Black Marks

John shares two other traits with his father: a quick wit and a penchant for pranks. He sent a stripper to meet with a co-worker who was interviewing prospective secretaries. "I thought she was a good candidate," the co-worker said, "more articulate than most."

Carried to extremes, pranks can reflect an underlying carelessness. But a friend justified what some might consider John's reckless behavior: "There's an incredible amount expected of John. He has to sacrifice what a lot of us would consider routine."

John has had several minor run-ins with the law. In 1988, he paid $2,300 in parking tickets. "I later learned the reason (he paid them)," recalled J. Bertrana Shair, the administrative judge who heard Kennedy's case. "He had to clear himself of all judgments in order to qualify for the D.A.'s office. I don't think he enjoyed writing the check. He said, in view of all the tickets, perhaps he ought to get free parking in the future." Shair gave him a gratuitous little lecture. "I told him he's going places. He should take care how he's perceived."

* * *

The blackest mark on Kennedy's record, though, is one that will be understood by anyone with a passing knowledge of the habits of 24-year-old men. Between 1984 and 1986, he and a friend sublet a co-op apartment on West 86th Street. According to an inside observer, Kennedy was often late with his rent checks and could never remember his keys. "He rang everyone's buzzer. He drove the super crazy. He had a water bed, which was against the rules. The board was within inches of evicting them."

Finally, their sublease ran out and the owner returned. "It looked like a herd of yaks had lived there," our informant continued. "Somebody had clearly put a fist through the wall. The carpet looked like they'd had cookouts on it. Every surface had to be sanded, spackled, and patched."

The current president of the building's co-op board is forgiving, though. "(Some) people tend to be tougher on personalities than on the rest of us."

An older and (presumably) wiser John Kennedy now lives alone in a two-bedroom apartment in the West Nineties, near Christina. He keeps his keys tied to his belt. Though his new apartment has been "nicely done" with his mother's decorating help, a friend says it is often "kind of messy."

In 1989, when finishing up his final year at NYU, he would often have breakfast at a health-food restaurant on Columbus Avenue and then bicycle ninety or so blocks south to the Greenwich Village campus. He also worked in Brooklyn Family Court, where, as a member of NYU's Juvenile Rights Clinic, he defended minors accused of felonies.

JFK "Kin Spirit"

Both John and his sister, Caroline Schlossberg, seem to be remarkably solid young people, given the circumstances of their lives. The credit is generally given to their mother, Jacqueline Onassis. Under unbearable scrutiny, she raised them amazingly well.

John has been a public curiosity since he was born. He gave out a "lusty cry" at birth, according to the obstetrician who delivered him by caesarean section on November 25, 1960. Seventeen days earlier, his father had been elected president. As the first White House baby since 1893, John Jr. made front pages around the world, but after his christening, his 31-year-old mother imposed a press blackout. The publicity-conscious president fought the blackout, with mixed success. He sneaked photographers and the kids into the Oval Office when Jackie was out of town, but no photos of John were released for a year.

Tidbits about him did leak out, though. In May 1963, he sucked his thumb while meeting astronaut Gordon Cooper, taking it out long enough to say "Cooper, Cooper." And in November 1963, at a Veterans Day program at Arlington National Cemetery, John-John, as he came to be called, upstaged the troops by performing acrobatics while dangling from the hands of his father and an aide. A few weeks later, the president boarded a helicopter at the White House for his fateful flight to Dallas. It was the last time the young son Jackie called "his real kin spirit" ever saw him.

Friends say that, though John rarely brings up his father, he is gracious when others do. Nevertheless, awkward moments do occur. "One time he was hanging out in somebody's room," recalled a fraternity brother, "and they were playing the Stones' 'Sympathy for the Devil' " (which contains the lyric "I shouted out, 'Who killed the Kennedys?'/When after all/it was you and me"). "Everyone realized, 'Uh-oh.' But at some point, he'd just walked out and then he walked back in again. He just avoided the situation."

Friends are careful with him. "(The assassination of his father) has never come up and I wouldn't bring it up," said Stevelman. "It can't be an easy thing. During the week of the (twenty-fifth) anniversary (of the assassination), I was worried for him. Who wants to be exposed to that? But he's incredibly together about it. I'm sure it moves him. How could it not? But he's integrating it into a sane life."

"I think he's very proud of what his father did," added another friend. "But he doesn't dwell on it. He'd probably prefer not to. John has very real memories, but when he talks with his sister and his mother, it's about real times, not Camelot. To us, JFK was a quasi-mythical figure. To him, it was his father."

The night his father died, John apparently learned the news at the Georgetown home of his grandmother Janet Auchincloss. John's third birthday party, planned for three days later in Hyannis Port, was delayed by the state funeral. During the services that day, the youngster looked bewildered until someone gave him a book to occupy him. Outside the cathedral, as the coffin passed by, John's mother whispered to him. He handed her the book and gave his father a perfect salute. Later, at the Capitol, he got restless and tried to pull away from Jackie, saying, "I want a flag to take home to my daddy."

Less than a year later, the Kennedys started a new life, moving into a sixteen-room park-view apartment at 1040 Fifth Avenue and renting a weekend retreat near Glen Cove, Long Island. They have always lived in luxurious homes and settings—from the Virginia hunt country to the Greek island of Skorpios. John's Secret Service code name, Lark, sums up his globe-trotting youth. Spring 1966, for example, found him in Hawaii, dividing his time between Laurance Rockefeller's ranch and industrialist Henry Kaiser's estate. When Kaiser's wife introduced him as John-John, he corrected her. "My name is not John-John," he said. "It's John."

A Difficult Age

He had reached a difficult age—six. At an August 1966 family wedding at Hammersmith Farm, the Auchincloss estate in Newport, John fought with his cousins, tried to chase ponies into the reception tent, and spattered bathers with sand on nearby Bailey's Beach. "That boy travels 90 miles an hour, at right angles to everyone else," noted a wedding guest.

In June 1968, his uncle Bobby, who had become a surrogate father to John, was also assassinated. Later that year, John was uprooted again when he switched schools. He left St. David's, a Roman Catholic school a few blocks away from 1040 Fifth, that he'd attended since nursery school, to enter the third grade at Collegiate, a 361-year-old unaffiliated Protestant school. The newspapers reported that he had been taken out of St. David's because the school wanted him to repeat the second grade. He was described as restless, disruptive, and inattentive. Jackie was said to have told him, "Don't worry about your spelling. Your father couldn't spell very well, either."

Perhaps another reason for his removal from a Roman Catholic school was his mother's impending remarriage—outside her church—to the Greek shipping magnate Aristotle Onassis. Their affair had blossomed that summer. Onassis spent a weekend at Hammersmith Farm with Jackie's mother, and then a few days with the children and grandmother Rose Kennedy in Hyannis Port. In October, just after Jackie and Onassis were wed on Skorpios, John and Caroline were sent home from Athens while their mother and Onassis honeymooned. Landing at John F. Kennedy International Airport, eight-year-old John frowned at photographers.

Onassis is said to have been a caring and generous stepfather. He invited Kennedy family and friends along on his and Jackie's summer voyages. "There was a kidding competition among our classmates to get to bicycle for a month on the deck of Ari's yacht," said a Collegiate pal of John's.

At the time, Jackie was said to consider the marriage to Onassis the perfect antidote to America's stifling fascination with her and her children. "If they're killing the Kennedys, then my children are targets," she said. "I want to get out of this country."

The threat was real. "There were bomb scares on at least two occasions," said the Collegiate classmate. "We all understood them to be Kennedy-related." There were also "these two characters in the office with their feet on the desk and underarm holsters, reading *The Daily News* all day," referring to John's Secret Service detail. "John didn't love (having) them following him around."

Aristotle Onassis died in Paris on March 15, 1975. Jackie's $26 million settlement with his estate, negotiated with Christina Onassis, added to established Kennedy trust funds and left the children without financial worries.

During the mid-seventies, John was listed in the Social Register. He was seeing a psychiatrist regularly, and changed schools again, transferring to Phillips Academy in Andover, Massachusetts. After being held back a year, he graduated in 1979. "He certainly wasn't at the top of his class," says a longtime friend.

John was known at all three private schools as bright, but more rebellious and troubled than Caroline. His most embarrassing teenage moment involved drinking. In 1978, he and Caroline celebrated their birthdays (his eighteenth, her twenty-first) with a bash at Le Club in New York, arranged by their mother. At five in the morning, as the party broke up, Kennedy and his school friends fought with a *National Enquirer* photographer. "I opened the door and John was lying in the gutter," recalled Patrick Shields, the club's director, who dusted him off and deposited him in a taxi. "Jackie's comment to me the next morning was 'I'm walking on a cloud.'" Shields didn't think she had seen the morning papers yet.

John also spent some time at Xenon, the club owned by Howard Stein, who called himself a "disco uncle" to the Kennedy cousins. They were treated like kings by Stein's partner, Peppo Vanini, who considered them "the closest thing to royals in America," Stein said. "We made overtures to induce them into our world."

Robert Kennedy's children became Xenon regulars, but "John was special," Stein remembered. "He was less a disco baby. He was shier, ingenuous. He didn't leverage his name the way kids of the famous do in my world. He had star quality. So every time he was there, he got his picture in the papers. It took a scandal for the other Kennedy kids to be photographed."

In the next half-dozen years, John would be photographed often in discos with a steady girlfriend, Sally Munro, who was in the class ahead of him at Brown. Ever the prankster, he identified her to photographers as "Lisa, my fiancée."

Nightlife wasn't the only temptation. Girls slept outside the door of his dorm room when he was a freshman. He later moved into the Phi Psi house and then into a house off campus that he shared with several students, including Christina Haag. Kennedy was also attracted to the stage, appearing in campus productions of *Volpone, Short Eyes* and *In the Boom-Boom Room*. Producer Robert Stigwood even offered John a part in a film, playing his father. He was interested, but his mother, reportedly, was upset.

The professional offers kept coming after he left Brown—"bad things, because of who he was," says Peter Allen. "He thought it would be fun, but he didn't want to trade on his name."

Show business remained alluring, though, and in the

summer of 1985, John finally appeared on a Manhattan stage, starring in six invitation-only performances of *Winners* at the 75-seat Irish Arts Center.

Kennedy and Christina Haag played star-crossed lovers in Northern Ireland, in a workshop mounted by friends from the drama set at Brown. Leaving the theater one night, John told a reporter, "This is not a professional acting debut. It's just a hobby." And reports varied on his talent. A Brown critic had once taken exception to his "prep-school voice."

Some time after the short run of *Winners,* John's relationship with Sally Munro ended amicably and Christina stepped into the role of girlfriend. "John had a secret crush on her since he was five," said a friend. "Actually, I don't think it was secret. He asked her out every week and she said no every time."

Friends say Haag is whimsical, stylish, and quite serious about her career—and that her relationship with John has not always helped it. But she never trades on him. Indeed, she avoids publicity that might help her. "They make her sound like a hanger-on," a friend says. "The fact is, her boyfriend takes away from her craft."

Friends admit that John and Christina have had some rough sledding. For a while after college, John "was playing around a lot," says a former co-worker. "He got along well with girls. He enjoyed it, like anyone would." But now, according to friends of Christina's, the relationship is strong. She even refers to herself as his "law widow."

An Impressive Résumé

Until now, no one has asked much of John Kennedy. But quietly, off the gossip pages, he has built an impressive résumé for a young man just starting his career. The summer before he went off to college, he attended the National Outdoor Leadership School with students from the United States and Africa, studying mountaineering and environmental issues 17,000 feet up Mount Kenya. The next summer, he met government and student leaders in Zimbabwe, and worked briefly for a mining company in Johannesburg. Maurice Tempelsman—Jackie's diamond merchant companion—probably had a hand in making the arrangement.

After his sophomore year at Brown, he worked for Ted Van Dyk at the Center for Democratic Policy, a Washington-based liberal think tank. Again, Tempelsman suggested that John apply for a student internship. Living with the Shrivers, John immersed himself in political organizing, advance work, research and working the room on a fund-raising trip to Hollywood. That summer, he recognized for the first time the power he had. "He began to realize he was a celebrity," said Van Dyk. "He had his first contact with clutchers and grabbers. He handled it."

John even talked back to Norman Lear, who, according to Van Dyk, "went on about what close friends he was with President Carter," and then said he was saving his money for his own lobbying group, People for the American Way. "You'd be better served giving the money to us," John was quoted as saying.

John was "genuinely undecided" about his future, and Van Dyk was sympathetic. "I get a churning stomach thinking about all those Kennedy kids in politics. I'm pleased to see them respond as several have, yet relieved when any of them decides to do something else. An expectation hangs over them. I don't think John feels compelled." Still, back at Brown, John worked for the University Conference for Democratic Policy, which sponsored disarmament forums on northeastern college campuses.

The summer after his junior year, Kennedy and his cousin Tim Shriver tutored underprivileged children in English as part of a University of Connecticut program.

After he graduated, he stopped for some fun, signing on as first mate on the *Vast Explorer,* searching for the pirate treasure ship *Whidah* in the waters off Cape Cod.

Following the 1984 Democratic Convention in San Francisco, where he helped Van Dyk raise funds, John came home and took a job with the city of New York. In his $20,000-a-year position in the Office of Business Development, he worked to attract and keep business in town. "His references were extraordinary," said his boss, Larry Kieves. "He worked in the same crummy cubbyhole as everyone else. I heaped on the work and was always pleased."

John "wasn't overly sophisticated," added a coworker. "He was one of the few young people there who acted his age," fondly recalling how he would change from his bicycle clothes into a suit in the office, but often leave his shirttail hanging out. (Though he still sometimes dresses that way, he was named to the International Best Dressed List this year.)

In 1986, John switched jobs, moving to the 42nd Street Development Corporation as acting deputy executive director, conducting negotiations with developers and city agencies. Jackie was on the nonprofit company's board. "John was an intelligent bargain," recalled Fred Papert, the corporation's president. "Salary was not of grave concern to him. He knew his way around the city. He's unpredictable in a good way. He was both orderly and passionate—a rare combination."

John entered law school that fall. The following summer, he worked for William Bradford Reynolds, the Reagan Justice Department's civil rights chief, making $358 a week as one of seven interns. In 1989, his salary improved when he became a $1,100-a-week summer associate at Manatt, Phelps, Rothenberg & Phillips, a Los Angeles law firm with strong Democratic Party connections, and worked for Charlie Manatt, Chairman of the Democratic National Committee.

At the 1988 Democratic Convention, major speakers chose the people who would introduce them. Ted Kennedy asked John, who was delighted. So was a party that was "trying to reach out to the younger boomer crowd," according to a Democratic National Committee official. Backstage, John "was nervous as hell," reported an observer. He needn't have worried. "Stars are born at conventions. He certainly came out as a Democrat everyone will be watching for a long time."

"A Real Mensch"

Does John want that? Friends and former employers say that he seems committed to some kind of public service. "He has a great way with people," says Andrew Cuomo, son of the governor of New York, who linked the Cuomo and Kennedy families through his marriage to Kerry Kennedy. "He's as comfortable with homeless kids in a playground as he is at the Democratic Convention, and that's truly a gift." In between law classes, he works with Cuomo's HELP Program, the Fresh Air Fund, the Kennedy Library, and the Kennedy Foundation's associate trustees. The foundation is behind his latest project: working with the City University of New York on a plan to assist the mentally handicapped. "He's not doing it to get recognition," says Dr. Jeffrey Sachs, who is working with John. "He's a real mensch."

His enthusiasm falters, it seems, only in academia. One of his NYU professors judged him unremarkable. "Given the opportunities offered someone so blessed, one would have wanted him to give more evidence of ambition, drive and vision. But maybe my course didn't inspire him."

Kennedy has apparently found something to inspire him in criminal law. And it isn't really surprising that a man whose father and uncle were both murdered should choose to become a prosecutor. The A.D.A.'s job is "tough work," according to law school friend

Stevelman. "It takes someone who really wants to get down and deal with real people's needs. I don't think John likes things easy or false."

"His interest in criminal law is marketable and useful," added a fellow law student. "He's not doing it for money reasons. He's very curious. He's interested and open. He's much more comfortable with black people, for instance, than your average kid of his world."

Before John ever appeared at the Brooklyn Family Court as a student lawyer, Joseph A. Esquirol Jr., the supervising judge, worried that the court would come to a stop. He recalled thinking that "every woman will leave her desk to come see him."

Concerned, Esquirol called his court staff together. "Don't make it any worse for him," he told them. "Try not to drool till he's gone. I want to give the young man a chance to grow in his profession. He has a right to that."

Drooling stenographers aren't the only obstacle Kennedy faces. "How would you feel, if you were a thirteen-year-old arrested for a chain-snatch, if the son of a president was your lawyer?" asks Esquirol, who has presided over three designated-felony cases in which John appeared. A fellow law student agreed. "(Who he is) comes up all the time. John presses it away and goes on."

NYU officials and teachers will not discuss Kennedy's grades, but Esquirol gives him high marks. "I don't know that he's the best or the worst," the judge said. "I don't envy him one minute. I think he can cut it if he's allowed to practice without pressure. He's got the innate common sense, ability, and presence. He knew what he was doing and why he was doing it. If I were a father, I wouldn't be disappointed to have him as a son."

John's work with the underprivileged and disabled, his experience bridging the public and private sectors, his inquisitive mind, sense of obligation, and his determination to avoid the obvious—a quick run for elective office—reveal a commendable sense of purpose. "He makes good decisions, not facile ones," says Stevelman. "He makes a point not to make broad decisions about life." It's not that he won't want our votes eventually. He just doesn't want them now, when all he would be is JFK II. But John F. Kennedy Jr. will always be America's son, and that's a hurdle he'll face for the rest of his life.

Another friend summed it up. "I honestly think in 100 years, they'll say that whatever he did, he succeeded not because he was John F. Kennedy Jr., but in spite of it."

CHAPTER TWO

THE CHILDREN OF
EUNICE KENNEDY
AND
SARGENT SHRIVER

Eunice Shriver (1921–) married R. Sargent Shriver, an attorney, the first director of the Peace Corps, and an unsuccessful vice-presidential candidate in 1972. She and her husband founded the Special Olympics in 1968.

Robert III (1954–)
Maria (1955–)
Timothy (1959–)
Mark (1964–)
Anthony (1965–)

Robert Sargent Shriver III
The Shriver Balance

While some Kennedys of this generation are picking up the political torch carried by their fathers and uncles, the flame of the Special Olympics torch burns in Bobby Shriver's heart. Robert Sargent Shriver III has been active in this family project for nearly all of his thirty-six years. His mother, Eunice, started this sports training and athletic program for people with mental disabilities, in 1968. She had experienced what such suffering could be like through her sister Rosemary, and was inspired to do something for others with the same affliction.

The seeds of the Special Olympics were sown at Timberlawn, an expansive summer home rented by his family. As a youngster, Bobby needed to do little more than step outside his door, to gain lessons in compassion. He lent a helping hand to what were then simple backyard activities involving fifty to sixty "kids" with mental retardation (actually ranging in age from five to sixty-five) who were annually invited to what became fondly known as "Camp Shriver." Bobby would often lead the opening ceremonies, gently showing some participants how to put their hands on their hearts as they listened to "The Star-Spangled Banner."

Today, while working professionally in New York City as a venture capitalist, Bobby still helps with what has grown into Special Olympics International, a program active in all fifty states, eighty countries, and involving over 750,000 participants.

As the eldest of his generation of Shrivers, Bobby inherited his family's desire to help others. "There is nothing *wrong* with being weak," he says. "But if you are strong, you should do something for those who aren't."

With the same rigor with which a political consciousness is ingrained in Kennedys, Bobby's parents raised their children to involve themselves in activities for others. For the children of Sargent and Eunice Shriver, charity to others truly began at home.

Bobby gained a great deal from both sides of his family—Kennedys and Shrivers. Describing his own father as "the greatest that ever lived," he was also deeply affected by the examples set by his more famous uncles. Unlike many of his cousins, Bobby was fortunate to come to adulthood without suffering the loss of a father's guidance and love. He could always come home to the security of two caring parents. And unlike the magnificent but often cold surroundings of many celebrity palaces, the Shriver house exuded warmth. With the exception of historical photographs perched on a baby grand piano and lining the walls, the home felt like that of any friendly neighbor.

The warmth extended beyond the immediate family to some of Bobby's cousins, who often sought out the Shrivers as a haven when they were in trouble or feeling lost amid so many children and too few parents. Eunice has earned a special place in many of their hearts as the adult who invariably came to their rescue. Supporting and caring, Bobby's mother wanted her children, nieces, and nephews to appreciate one another as unique and special. When Bobby's sister, Maria, was starting out in her television career, Eunice gave her other children miniature portable televisions so that wherever they were, they could watch Maria's morning news show.

The interlocking protectiveness of the Kennedy family is such that no outsider may disturb one link without having to deal with the reaction of the entire chain. However, intramural rivalries are accepted, often expressed through playful yet sometimes serious teasing.

The children of the Kennedy *women* were a regular target of the taunts of cousins who were blessed with the "right" last name. Riding in the front seat, getting the first dessert, or getting the first hug from Grandma Rose was sometimes touted by the children of John, Robert, and Ted as being reserved for the "real Kennedys" . . . not for Shrivers, Lawfords, or Smiths. In their earlier years, Bobby and Ethel's kids in particular would push themselves ahead of their "no-name" cousins, declaring: "Me first, *I'm* a Kennedy!"

However, spirited Shrivers would show pride in *their* name. When asked if not having the Kennedy name suggested a form of second-class citizenship within the clan, Bobby retorted, with Kennedy *vigor*, "Absolutely not!" The standard within *his* family, established by *his* father, is that Shrivers get equal billing.

Of course, it was not the name that was important, but the person behind the name. Bobby's parents have very different, yet complementary styles. His mother, with Kennedy directness, would usually tell her children what to do. His father's method, on the other hand, was to take the time to draw answers out of them. As an intellectual, Sargent wanted his children first to value the thought process, reasoning their way through a problem.

Bobby's father also provided emotional strength. To the assertive masculine Kennedy competitiveness, the Shrivers added caring and sensitivity. Whether apocryphal or not, an oft-repeated story illustrates a distinction between the Shriver and Kennedy families. As the story goes, one of the Shriver boys was slugged by one of his cousins and began to cry. He was promptly admonished—by a Kennedy—that "Kennedys don't cry." At the same moment Sargent Shriver happened on the scene. The former vice-presidential candidate counseled his son, "You are a Shriver, and Shrivers *can* cry."

Though one account of this story has Bobby as the victim, a grown-up Bobby said, "I don't remember who it was, but that *is* something my father would say."

Wearing Many Hats

A Kennedy, of course, yet this Shriver is intent upon also living up to and promoting his father's side of the family. Coincidentally, the name "Shriver" is an Anglicization of the German name, "Schreiber," which means "writer," the profession that Bobby initially pursued, putting in several years as a newspaper reporter. Beginning as an intern at what is now the *Annapolis Capitol,* in Maryland, he impressed managing editor Tom Marquardt as "the only reporter who wore shorts to work—and got away with it." Marquardt also recalls that Bobby was determined to establish himself as a good reporter —not just a Kennedy who was also a reporter. "He fit right in with the other writers and never bragged about his obvious status in life."

While in Maryland, a still-young Bobby was caught hawking Orioles tickets outside Memorial Stadium in Baltimore. Years later, ironically, he handled the legalities of his father's successful effort to buy a percentage of the team.

After leaving Annapolis, Bobby went on to Chicago and eventually landed a job with the *Chicago Daily News,* predecessor to today's *Sun-Times.* But Chicago wasn't far enough west for him, so he continued in that direction, writing for a time for the now-defunct *Los Angeles Herald.* Although he enjoyed the California lifestyle, he ultimately decided New York was where he really wanted to be. Though his office is in Manhattan, Bobby sees well beyond the city's borders. Through his involvement in his father's, uncle's, and cousins' political campaigns, Bobby knows the political side of the nation from the inside out, and has travelled all over the world through the Special Olympics.

In addition to serving on the executive committee of the board of directors of Special Olympics International, Inc., he also works tirelessly (and for free) with

Special Olympics Productions, a separate company within the corporation that holds the copyrights to television shows, records, and other entertainment ventures that benefit or showcase the Special Olympics. Bobby explains that he would never have succeeded with some large fund-raising efforts without his business knowledge and experience. A record album entitled "A Very Special Christmas," initiated by Jimmy and Vickie Iovine and realized with Bobby's help, has made $15 million since its debut in 1987. Production work is another area of great interest for Bobby, enhanced greatly when the end result brings money in for his family's cause. "The difference in charity promotions," Bobby explains, "is that in most cases, you'll read on charity invitations to dinners or other charity albums, that a portion of the proceeds will go to that charity. In our case, with this album, all of the proceeds go to Special Olympics. Everyone worked for free." From Madonna and other star performers on down to the sound man and record producer, people donated their time and talents, an unusual example of true philanthropy in today's world of opportunistic fund-raising.

Although philanthropy is a consuming interest in Bobby's life, with Special Olympics in his heart, it is making money that is very much on Bobby's mind. In the spirit of his grandfather, he sees obtaining wealth as a challenge and a necessity. For some, it may be a deterrent to realize that it takes money to make money, but Bobby's object is to parlay an old fortune into a new one.

Thus, after his earlier years as a journalist, and following a very brief stint as an attorney, Bobby moved into the world of venture capital. He cut his capitalist teeth working for another firm, then moved out on his own, where on a volunteer basis he also puts his expertise in raising money to work for the benefit of the Special Olympics.

Bobby has no qualms about enjoying the pursuit of money—far from it. "Understanding money is a very useful thing," he says. He also suggests that he is one Kennedy heir who actually *has* to work, at least to maintain the lifestyle of the rich and famous. He says circumspectly, yet clearly, "Certain (of the Kennedy) heirs have different relationships to different amounts of money; and certain others added up that money and decided that they'd better go out and get a job. If you notice, all of the Shriver children are working—and need their salaries."

Lessons Learned

Bobby is now secure in his quest to blend his personal success with his passion for helping the afflicted, but his road was not always smooth. His adolescence was not unlike that of some of his troubled cousins, with whom he often hung out. He was once even arrested for possession of marijuana, an incident that helped convince him to take life more seriously. He still believes in having fun, but balances it with responsibility. He doesn't wish to erase any of his mishaps, however, saying, "It is all of one's experiences that creates the person that you become."

Tall, handsome, a Kennedy, and still a bachelor, Bobby has become one of America's most eligible. He continues to enjoy the company of many beautiful and talented women, but according to a longtime friend, Richard Plepler, Bobby is "still looking for that very special person . . . the *right* person . . . as we all are."

Bobby also enjoys tennis. As a child, this was the one game in which he could beat his more rough and tumble, football-oriented cousins. Clearly, Bobby prefers to be seen as a winner. However, these days one area where he *always* loses (according to Plepler) is when the two face each other on the tennis court.

With friends and family he may accept defeat graciously, but maintaining an appearance of humility—when fame, fortune, and good looks have smiled so warmly upon him—is difficult for Bobby at times. More than a few people have experienced Bobby's masterful use of the art of intimidation.

Many of his famous cousins recognized the value of their situations early, and started taking advantage of it. They sold Kennedy sand and Kennedy grass to gullible tourists in Hyannis Port, and answered questions about their parents, aunts, and uncles—for a price.

As described in the book, *The Kennedys*, a young David Kennedy was once asked what it meant to be a Kennedy, to which he replied, "It means that we're exactly like everyone else, except better."

On occasion, Bobby has acted out his late cousin's description of a Kennedy. He once balked at having the organizer of a major Special Olympics fund raiser introduced with the likes of Robin Leach, Brooke Shields, Pia Zadora and Robert Sargent Shriver III. The woman was merely a Special Olympics staffer and not a big name. Bobby decided to do something about this problem, and told the director to substitute someone of greater status as the key person behind the event. An annoyed director advised Bobby that the organizer of the event had worked hard for his family's cause for three years and that this particular affair would not have taken place without her. Digging in his heels, he insisted that if Bobby would not introduce her, he would. A chastened Bobby proceeded onto the stage himself and offered an eloquent introduction.

Though from a famous family, Bobby does not seek the spotlight for himself. Initially, he sought to avoid an interview for this book. Finally, he relented to a brief conversation, and then gave, with resistance, an hour and a half. Bobby takes the position that he's not a politician, athlete, or performer and has done nothing particularly of public interest. "I'm not a public figure," he says, "and I don't deserve publicity." Little has been written about him, and he "prefers it that way."

Though reluctant to talk about himself, and with a politician's adeptness at parrying probing questions with unrevealing answers, Bobby becomes talkative when the focus turns from him to the Special Olympics. The conversation is interrupted only once, when he decides to take a call. "It's a lawyer, and I *always* accept calls from lawyers," he says half-jokingly. A lawyer himself, a graduate of Yale Law School, his father's alma mater, Bobby is establishing his own star in the Kennedy firmament.

Although he laces his Kennedyesque charm and savvy with a tinge of sarcasm borne of a patrician's self-confident view of the world, he is a shining example of this generation of Kennedys. A very careful person, scrupulously discreet, Bobby is quietly yet forcefully emerging as a Kennedy on the move. But political ambitions? Not at the moment. It is noteworthy, however, that while keeping a low public profile, he is building an impressive political base.

Whatever his present or future endeavors—capitalist, philanthropic, political—Bobby Shriver is shaped for success. However, the Kennedy creed to be strong and to win is balanced by the Shriver credo that is succinctly described in the Special Olympics oath:

> Let me win
> But if I cannot win
> Let me be brave
> In the attempt.

Maria Shriver

The News Breaker

Daughter of an unsuccessful vice-presidential candidate . . . niece of Jack, Bobby and Ted Kennedy . . . wife of bodybuilder turned movie star Arnold Schwarzenegger . . . mother of a one-year-old baby. That might be enough for many women, but not for Maria Shriver—she's also a television journalist for NBC.

It was 8:00 a.m. one morning a few years ago. Maria had just jetted in to Los Angeles airport from New Mexico, where she and her husband were "just hanging out" on the set of his latest movie. At breakfast in the airport cafeteria, she wore no makeup, but her mischievous green eyes and jaw with the sweeping lines of a racing sloop gave her a strong, spectacular beauty. "As I get older it becomes more wrenching every time I have to leave Arnold," she said, unconsciously twisting her hair into a braid. "I like to be home. I think if I didn't have to work I could just stay there—but then what?"

Today, she is home much of the time. That's where she produces *Cutting Edge with Maria Shriver,* devoting nearly all day Monday through Friday. She likes this kind of life-style. "I've heard from so many women who said, 'Thank God, I can now work to a certain point and still have the option down the road of having a family.' "

Unlike her earlier shows, this one is an interview show designed to her own specifications. Instead of going to a star's hotel room to do a long dragged-out affair in front of pretty flowers, she prefers to capture people at their work—at doing what makes them famous. A recent interview profiled Irish pop singer Sinead O'Connor sitting on the floor in a warehouse (where the singer obviously felt comfortable) and television star Kirstie (*Cheers*) Alley going about her daily business.

Another reason she is so happy with this kind of format is that it's a morning show. "Morning television puts me right into a viewer's bedroom. They decide whether or not they want me there. If they don't they'll flip the channel and throw me out."

The pink denim dress she had on that day in Los Angeles was one she'd worn before on camera and would wear again in a couple of hours when the NBC car delivered her to a location shoot nearby. "Sure, I wear things more than once, just like people in regular life do," she said, biting into a bran muffin.

As a member of that glamorous, high-achieving clan the whole word knows as The Kennedys, Maria Shriver is determined to distinguish herself as an individual. She admits that her family found her choice to cross over to the news side a bit odd, but says they have been very supportive of her determination to be her own woman. She worked hard for the last fourteen years climbing the treacherous ladder of television news. Before adding to her family, she co-hosted *Sunday Today*, a weekly news and information program, and solos on *Main Street*, a monthly news show aimed at young people.

She once made ten international trips in five months, including a particularly horrendous week in which she flew to Israel and back to Los Angeles. But that was just the beginning. The next day, she was airborne again, bound this time for Jordan, then to New York, and back to Jordan again before finally returning home to L.A. Although she doesn't believe in jet lag, she admitted that that week got to her.

"Every time I made those fifteen-hour flights, I came home sick. One night I had what I thought was whooping cough, and spent the whole night driving around New York trying to find Nyquil."

Ever since the age of sixteen, she was possessed by

the ambition to make her mark in television journalism. In those days, of course, she was on the other side of the fence. Her father was running for vice president, and she often traveled with him. But she found she preferred the back of the plane to the front, because that was where the press traveled. "I thought they were bright and had a job where they were learning all the time, and I liked their sense of camaraderie."

Playing by Most Family Rules

"My mother is tough as nails—a great mother and a great woman, very independent. She's constantly pushing and challenging herself and has told me that much has been given me and therefore I should do something with it."

Maria grew up believing that she could do anything a man could do, and the same rules that applied to her brothers applied to her—with one exception: dating. "I was watched like a hawk and had to get in at midnight." She had only two boyfriends—one from sophomore year in high school through junior year in college, and the second in college. And then came Arnold. . . .

Though she met him shortly after finishing Georgetown, it took them seven years to marry. "I thought he was interesting and I was impressed by his sense of humor. But I was embarking on a television job in Philadelphia. I had to block a lot of other stuff out for a time because it was important for me to find something on my own and excel at it. I grew up in a family where everybody excelled.

"I wanted to feel that I was making my own life and that I was O.K. with me before I could expect someone else to buy into me." But she demurred when asked whose idea it was to tie the knot. "I don't even tell my mother those sorts of things," she said, bursting into girlish giggles as she flipped off the tape recorder.

Maria often originates her ideas based on her own

experience, and then expands them to focus on the larger social issues involved. "When I had to get around in a cast, it made me aware of how difficult life is for the handicapped," for example. And on the subject of privacy: "I come from a public family. I work in a public profession, my husband's in a public profession, and I am therefore public, too. But that doesn't mean everything in my life is public."

Four years ago Arnold and Maria were married in Hyannis Port in a big wedding with heavy media coverage. Maria says she spent eight months planning it. More than eighty members of her family and more than a few of the famous were in attendance. But there was a snafu: she had broken her toe in an accident a few days before and had to switch to sneakers in order to dance. Her wedding ring is the size of an auto headlight, and she has a habit of twisting it backward as she speaks.

The couple moved into a Mediterranean-style house in Pacific Palisades, a relaxed, family-oriented community near the ocean in Los Angeles, complete with pool and tennis courts and two Labradors, Conan and Strudel. She reluctantly gave up her old Capri with its Georgetown sticker ("I was so emotionally attached to it, but it's bad to get attached to material things"), and won't say what she's driving now. She works out at least an hour a day in the gym, eats mostly chicken and fish, rarely drinks anything alcoholic and maintains a low social profile. She and Arnold enjoy dinner out with friends or riding their horses—he saddles up his Andalusian the Western way, while she prefers to ride her hunter English style. They play tennis and ski during Christmas in Aspen. "It's a nice life, boringly normal, like anybody else's," she insists. Although of course, it isn't.

Although Arnold's public image is that of a movie jock, friends know him as an intelligent, civilized man with a delightful sense of humor, who earned a handsome salary in real estate long before he struck it rich in the movies. "Arnold is very warm and family-oriented, but he combines that with a great sense of drive. He is also very goal-oriented, so he accepts that in me." Mutual admiration.

A Series of Goals Achieved

"I noticed during the 1972 campaign that people were learning about the candidates from television, and I realized it was becoming a medium to be reckoned with. So when I made up my mind, I put on blinders and just went." In 1982, she decided to switch from being a producer to reporting on air, and approached a Hollywood agent, asking him to represent her.

The reaction she got was unexpected. "You look like crap. I wouldn't represent you if you were the last person in the world. Lose weight and get your act together," she was told. "I was so shocked that I did." She lost forty pounds and polished her presentation techniques. "I worked on my diction because I always talked too fast and didn't finish my words. I had to stop using my big Irish family hands, and to learn to develop a thought in fifteen seconds instead of fifteen minutes."

Then she set about to achieve her next goal—to become a network anchor by the age of thirty. She shut out all distractions and took only five days vacation a year. She reflects that "growing up with a lot of opportunities can make or break people because it can be hard to focus. If I think, well, I'll go on this vacation over Christmas, and then away with my family over Easter, and then take a few weeks with them at the Cape, people won't think I'm serious. So when someone would suggest a trip, I wouldn't even listen. It's very hard to refuse, especially when the reason is not the rent check."

Clearly, Maria has taken the family competitive spirit to heart. "I remember being brought up always to win, to be Number One, but when I'm thinking about that all the time and don't succeed, it can be overwhelming and defeating."

She reached her next goal, but almost immediately failed. The *CBS Morning Show,* her first network position, was canceled after one run. "I was angry. I thought I was behaving in a responsible way and not trying to stick it to people, but they stuck it to me in the most brutal way."

Her firing was painful partly because it was so very public, and partly because although some people were very supportive, others didn't say anything. "Van Sauter never spoke to me about it—never, ever. I was raised believing I should try to do unto others as I would have them do unto me."

Yet, typically, Maria finds these struggles redeeming. "When I went through all the fears of problems that could occur and survived them, it was liberating. I didn't fear things anymore and gained confidence.

"Yes, I am a fatalist. I believe that things—good and bad—happen for a reason. I guess I got that from my grandmother, who said God would never give me what I couldn't handle. Life goes on. Things happen, and I accept them, assuming I will benefit, grow, and learn from them."

Maria has had her triumphs too. She did not get her exclusive interviews with Fidel Castro or Corazon Aquino simply by being a Kennedy. "It's a business. They want to be on the show with the biggest audience," she said, matter-of-factly.

The Philippine president struck Maria as someone who is totally without fear. "She told me her husband had been in prison for eight years and nothing could ever be that bad again." As for the Cuban leader, Maria commented, "I had been curious about him since I was old enough to think his history was so intertwined with that of my family. But we didn't sit around and discuss old times. I didn't go there to become friends—I went to interview him."

Asked about her private feelings about her place in the historic Kennedy-Castro confrontation, Maria bristled politely. "Yes, I had private thoughts; but that's why they're called 'private.' We all ask so many things that are, quote, Kennedy-related, unquote, and I don't look at things that way. I go through what I'm doing today and I don't think about the personal historical stuff ever."

How, then, does Maria Shriver see herself? "As a woman, Maria Shriver: married, working, blessed with a wonderful family, with parents I love."

And her goals? "Just getting through the day. Now I just want to survive and do good work. When people ask me where I'll go now, I say, 'This is O.K. I'm happy right here—just let me stay put for a while.'"

Timothy Shriver

"An extraordinary young man—a saint in some ways." Those are the words a close Kennedy observer uses to describe Timothy Perry Shriver. The third child of Eunice Kennedy and R. Sargent Shriver, Timothy was born on August 29, 1959. His brother Robert was five years old when he was born, and his sister, Maria, was four. His brothers Mark and Anthony were born five and six years later. So Timothy was truly a middle child. Although great pals with his brothers and sisters, John Kennedy Jr. has always been one of his best friends.

Timothy's home life was nurturing and challenging. Eunice, a consummate Kennedy, and Sargent, an independent intellectual and successful businessman, had somewhat different but very compatible philosophies. The Kennedy brand of Irish Catholicism was tempered by Shriver's German Catholicism—equally devout, but more intellectually based. They were dedicated and concerned parents. Eunice emphasized excellence in school and in sports; Sargent, no mean athlete himself, stressed the intellectual, theological and philosophical aspects of his children's development.

Timothy attended St. Alban's School in Washington, D.C., and during the summers often went with his family to the Kennedy compound in Massachusetts. However, for more than a decade, five weeks of each summer were devoted to the day camp that his mother ran on the grounds of the Shrivers' home in rural Maryland, which served fifty to sixty people with mental retardation. Timothy's grandparents, Joseph and Rose Fitzgerald Kennedy, founded the Joseph P. Kennedy Jr. Memorial Foundation in memory of their son, a navy pilot who was killed in World War II, to help others like their daughter Rosemary, who was born mentally retarded. When Eunice saw the ways that her campers seemed to flourish and improve, she decided to expand the program and founded Special Olympics, under the auspices of the Foundation. Special Olympics has expanded throughout the United States and the world. In recognition of her outstanding work for the mentally and physically disabled, President Ronald Reagan awarded Eunice the Medal of Freedom, the highest honor given to civilians.

After graduating from St. Alban's in 1977, Timothy followed his older brother to Yale University, their father's alma mater. Always deeply motivated by his religion and concern for others, after he received his degree in 1981, Timothy worked briefly in the high school equivalency program at a prison in Lorton, Virginia. From there he returned to New Haven, where he held two jobs: one working with sexually abused children; the other, working with Upward Bound, a precollegiate program designed to enhance the academic and social skills of disadvantaged adolescents to enable them to complete high school and go on to college.

Timothy spent a year on a Field Foundation fellowship at the Yale Child Study Center, working on programs for school reform and improvement. In 1987 he earned his master's degree in religion and education.

In 1986 Timothy married Linda Potter, a lawyer active in politics. She was a childhood friend of Timothy's cousin Courtney Kennedy and had interned in his uncle's Senate office. Although Timothy and Linda had known each other for many years, they didn't start dating until much later. They now live in New Haven with their daughter, Rose Potter Shriver, born in 1987, and their son, Timothy Potter Shriver, born a year later.

Timothy is the director of a special social development project of the New Haven public school system.

He coordinates programs for at-risk youths, and focuses on improving the school environment and developing strategies that will encourage these students to stay in school and to avoid self-defeating behavior such as drug and alcohol use, and teenage pregnancy. Timothy has always stressed that the benefits of these programs extend to both the students and their teachers, and that he considers his work "a mutual learning experience."

When asked if he has any plans to enter politics, his answer was an unqualified no. He said, "I can't say what I'll do for the rest of my life; I live one day at a time. But this is my profession and my work is here. I find it interesting and fulfilling, I learn a lot, and I think I'm being helpful."

Mark Shriver

Mark Kennedy Shriver keeps one of the lowest profiles of all the Kennedy cousins. The fourth of the five children of Eunice Kennedy and R. Sargent Shriver, he was born on February 17, 1964.

With his older brothers as role models, his athletic skills were sharpened during summers at Hyannis Port. Mark became an outstanding athlete at an early age, and helped coach at the summer camp for people with mental retardation that his mother opened at her home each year. When the camp evolved into the Special Olympics, Mark became a highly active member of the team of volunteers that is an essential part of the organization.

Mark attended Georgetown Prep, a private school for boys outside Washington, from which he graduated in 1982. He worked summers for the Baltimore Orioles, a baseball team then owned by lawyer Edward Bennett Williams. He then went on to Holy Cross College where he played competitive rugby. In 1986, after he received his Bachelor of Arts from Holy Cross, Mark headed for Baltimore, where he helped his cousin Kathleen Kennedy Townsend's campaign to become representative to Congress from Maryland.

Mark found that he liked living in his father's native state and decided to settle in Baltimore. Sensing a need, Mark initiated, obtained funding for and continues to operate *Choice,* a program for troubled teenagers and juvenile offenders in Baltimore's inner city. He still lends his efforts to his family's many public service projects and serves on the board of directors of Maryland Special Olympics.

Although he appears unlikely to pursue a career in politics, Mark Shriver unquestionably shares many of the concerns that are his heritage: to be of service and to be loyal, generous and kind.

Anthony Shriver

While a senior at Georgetown University in 1987, Anthony Shriver organized and founded Best Buddies of America, Inc., a nonprofit organization designed to provide opportunities for college students and people with mild to moderate mental retardation to become friends. Headquartered in Washington, D.C., Best Buddies has rapidly established regional offices in Los Angeles, Chicago and New York City, and now operates chapters at 67 college and university campuses nationwide.

Anthony has always been influenced by his mother's drive to help others. The youngest of the five children of Eunice Kennedy and Robert Sargent Shriver Jr. was born on July 20, 1965. When Anthony was three years old, President Lyndon B. Johnson named Sargent Shriver U.S. Ambassador to France. The Shrivers encouraged their children to speak French during the two years they were there. When the family returned to the United States, Anthony had forgotten much of his English. His mother enrolled him in a special program in Baltimore and made it a point to read English with Anthony each evening.

The Shrivers often joined the rest of the Kennedy family at Hyannis Port. But for ten years, many weeks of each summer were devoted to the camp for individuals with mental retardation that Eunice operated at their family home in Maryland. This project later developed into Special Olympics International.

Like his older brother Mark, Anthony attended Georgetown Prep and graduated in 1984. At Georgetown University he majored in theology and history. After receiving his degree in 1988, Anthony began working as the full-time volunteer president for Best Buddies.

He is also a representative of Special Olympics International, for which he has evaluated programs throughout the nation and worldwide.

A contemporary of his says, "Anthony is the most caring and giving person imaginable. He's always helping others. When he was in the Big Brothers program, he really was that little kid's best friend." Though seldom in the news, Anthony is very outgoing and leads an active social life. He is part of the cousins group that includes Mark Shriver, Patrick Kennedy and Max, Douglas and Rory Kennedy. When describing Anthony, those who know him well say that he is "gregarious, handsome, athletic, very committed and incredibly nice."

CHAPTER THREE

THE CHILDREN OF PATRICIA KENNEDY AND PETER LAWFORD

Patricia Lawford (1921–) Her marriage to actor Peter Lawford ended in divorce in 1965. She has not remarried.

Christopher (1955–)
Sydney (1956–)
Victoria (1958–)
Robin (1961–)

Christopher Lawford

Two things stand out in Christopher Lawford's mind about the period after his parents were divorced: his mother's insistence that he and his sisters stay in touch with their father, and the extra time and attention his uncles devoted to helping him adjust.

Christopher Kennedy Lawford was born on March 29, 1955, the first child of Patricia Kennedy and actor Peter Lawford. Christopher and his three younger sisters lived in Santa Monica, California, until their parents divorced in 1965, when Patricia moved with the children to New York.

After his early schooling, Christopher entered Middlesex School in Concord, Massachusetts. During summer vacations at the Kennedy compound on Cape Cod, the good-looking, bright and athletic Chris readily made friends with his cousins.

Chris found it difficult to reconcile the Hollywood world of his father with the political focus of the rest of his family. As an adult, he seems comfortable with both, but during adolescence, trying to make sense of the assassinations of his uncles added to his trepidation about being able to live up to their legacy.

Like several of his cousins, Chris turned to drugs. For ten years he was involved in escapades that attracted negative media attention. Although he continued to participate in volunteer work for the Very Special Arts, which his aunt, Jean Kennedy Smith, had founded for mentally and physically disabled children, he was struggling to deal with his own disorder. Throughout his problem period, when he was in and out of drug programs, his mother and sisters offered constant support. Eunice Shriver also took a special interest in Chris and sought to help him gain self-confidence. Unlike many Kennedys, who cloak their feelings with stoicism, Chris openly admitted his need to work through his emotions.

When Chris attended Tufts University, he worked as a summer intern in his uncle Ted's Senate office. After the Lawfords' divorce, Ted regarded Chris as one of his special responsibilities and made a point of including him in family camping trips and of being with him on significant occasions.

After graduating from Tufts in 1976, Chris seemed indecisive about his future. Former U.S. Attorney General Ramsey Clark, a family friend, put him to work in his unsuccessful campaign for the U.S. Senate and convinced him to consider law as a career.

Chris entered law school at Boston College and earned his degree in 1983. While there, he developed a friendship with Jeannie Olsson, a journalist of Swedish-Korean descent, who became assistant to the head coach of the Boston Breakers in the subsequently disbanded U.S. Football League. According to Chris, she was his support system during law school and he couldn't have made it without her.

Chris and Jeannie Olsson were married in May 1984. They are the parents of David Christopher Lawford, born in 1987, and Savannah Rose Lawford, born in 1990. They live in Pacific Palisades, California. Jeannie is a full-time mother.

For now, at least, Chris has gravitated back more to the paternal side of his roots, developing his skills and résumé as a film actor. He also makes time to work in the Very Special Arts program and to counsel young people with drug problems.

Sydney Lawford

As John F. Kennedy lay in state at the U.S. Capitol, seven-year-old Sydney Lawford leaned against her father, his hand on her long blond hair. Two years later, Sydney moved East from California, after her parents' divorce. Then in 1968, twelve-year-old Sydney suffered another loss, when her Uncle Bobby was assassinated.

Pat Lawford was an energetic single parent, and encouraged her children to memorize poems, read avidly and excel in their studies. She took them to museums, galleries, concerts, and plays, determined that the Kennedy penchant for excellence would be passed on to her children.

During summers at their grandparents' home at Hyannis Port, though the young Lawfords were encouraged to be competitive and athletic, the girls did not develop the kinds of rivalries that united and divided their male cousins. Sydney's closest friends among the cousins were—and still are—Maria Shriver, Caroline Kennedy and Courtney Kennedy, all about the same age. Sydney, with her keen sense of humor, is considered the comic of the group.

After her early schooling, she was enrolled in Foxcroft, an exclusive girls school in the Hunt Country of Virginia, known for its emphasis on horsemanship. A strikingly good-looking young woman, Sydney gravitated toward fashion. After graduating from Tobe Coburn Fashion Institute in 1978, Sydney's first job was at Jordan Marsh, Boston's top department store, which she subsequently left to enter marketing and advertising.

While working in Boston, Sydney met TV producer Peter McKelvey, whom she married in September 1983.

The McKelveys now live in Chevy Chase, Maryland and have three sons: Peter Jr., Patrick and Christopher. Sydney is famous in her family for keeping track of birthdays and anniversaries and for being ready to host a celebration whenever she finds the slightest excuse.

Victoria Lawford

When Pat Kennedy became involved with British actor Peter Lawford, her father openly opposed the
match. Nevertheless, the Lawfords were married in
1954, and over the next six years had four children. Observers said that although they appeared very much in
love, Pat always seemed more Kennedy than Lawford.
They were divorced in 1965. Lawford, who had lent welcome glamor to the presidential campaign and the Camelot years of John F. Kennedy, remained close to the
family until his death.

Victoria Frances Lawford, their third child and second daughter, was born on November 4, 1958, the day
her uncle John F. Kennedy was reelected to the United
States Senate.

When, after the divorce, Patricia and her children
moved from California to New York, Victoria adjusted
to winters in Manhattan and summers at the Kennedy
compound in Massachusetts and Southhampton, where
her mother has a home. Patricia was determined to help
compensate her children for the distance from their father by encouraging their closeness with their aunts, uncles and cousins. While it was a given that all the
Kennedys would participate in athletics, it was understood that the girls would be less competitive than the
boys. However, in the case of Victoria and her cousin
Kerry, sparks reportedly flew sometimes. They are good
friends now, but the family still laughs about the day the
two preteen girls got into a hair-pulling match as their
respective brothers and sisters cheered them on and
other cousins took sides.

Victoria graduated from Lyceé Francais, a private
school for girls in New York, in 1976. From there she

went to Mount Vernon College in Washington, D.C., where, in 1981, she received a B.A. in Arts and Humanities. Victoria has always particularly valued her friendship with her Uncle Ted. She has worked in his campaigns and often sought his guidance and encouragement. When she was at college in Washington, they became even closer.

After college, Victoria's job search lasted for eighteen months. Employers didn't think a Kennedy would be willing to start at the bottom and stick to a job, but Victoria persisted and was eventually hired by a cable television company. She became a production assistant for C-Span, a public affairs television network. She later left C-Span to join the staff of the Washington office of her Aunt Jean Kennedy's Very Special Arts program, where she worked on television productions for that project. She remained there until just before the birth of her first child.

Victoria is married to Robert Pender, an attorney in private practice in Washington, D.C. They have two children: Alexandra, born in March, 1987 and Caroline, born in May, 1990.

Robin Lawford

The youngest child of Patricia Kennedy and Peter Lawford, Robin Elizabeth Lawford was born on July 2, 1961. Her godfather was then-Attorney General Robert F. Kennedy. Peter and Pat Lawford were very much a part of two worlds—the glamor of Hollywood and the inner circle of Washington.

Robin's three older siblings were protective of the little redhead. After her parents divorced—when she was four—the vivacious Robin was brought east by her mother and adapted easily to her bevy of assertive cousins.

Patricia Lawford tried to protect her children from the media attention that went with being a Kennedy. While her mother didn't always succeed in keeping the paparazzi away, Robin has maintained a comparatively low profile. After her 1980 graduation from Unis School in New York, Robin enrolled in Marymount College in Manhattan. When she graduated in 1984, she followed an early interest in the theater and set out to find work. She became a stage manager for off-Broadway shows, but found she preferred the casting aspects of production. Robin has also been involved with other family projects, particularly Very Special Arts.

Robin dates and has many friends, and counts her sisters, her brother, and her Kennedy cousins as among her favorite companions.

CHAPTER FOUR

THE CHILDREN OF ETHEL SKAKEL

AND

ROBERT KENNEDY

Robert F. Kennedy (1925–1968) served as U.S. Attorney General during the administration of his brother and was elected U.S. Senator from New York in 1964. He was a candidate for president in 1968 until he was assassinated. His wife is the former Ethel Skakel, whose roots were in the Chicago area. Ethel has not remarried.

Kathleen (1951–)

Joseph II (1952–)

Robert Jr. (1954–)

David (1955–1984)

Courtney *Max*
(1956–) *(1965–)*
Michael *Douglas*
(1958–) *(1967–)*
Kerry *Rory*
(1959–) *(1968–)*
Christopher
(1963–)

Kathleen Kennedy Townsend
A Winner Who Lost

Kennedys never lose. They don't lose at touch football, they don't lose bets, and they never (well, hardly ever) lose elections.

That's why that November morning in 1986 was so bitter for Kathleen Kennedy Townsend, the eldest child of Robert and Ethel Kennedy. She had reached for the brass ring, and missed. She could have spared herself the pain and embarrassment by starting at the beginning of the electoral road, vying for a local office instead of Congress. But she was confident. She was stubborn. She was a Kennedy.

However, she underestimated her opponent. Freshman Congresswoman Helen Delich Bentley of the 2nd Maryland Congressional District was no pushover. Bentley had proved her mettle during her quarter century as waterfront reporter for the *Baltimore Sun*. After being named the first female maritime newspaper editor in the nation, she went on to become the first female chairman of the Federal Maritime Commission. It took her three consecutive tries to win her seat, and this daughter of a Nevada coal miner was not about to relinquish it easily—not even to a Kennedy.

Strong-willed and determined, Kathleen was certain she had a chance to break into national politics, despite her inexperience, and would brook no disagreement from her family. After all, she was the oldest of her generation, the first Kennedy woman to ever consider running for public office. Never mind that she had three young children at home. She had a mission, and she was going to achieve it.

She knocked on some 14,000 doors throughout the

district, even jumping over fences when she couldn't find an easier way in. Observers noted that she was "tireless," and commended her for not trading on her maiden name. She ran as a Townsend and introduced herself that way. Leslie Hutchinson went door-to-door with Kathleen during the general campaign in Essex, Maryland, and remembers her as one of the hardest campaigners she had ever seen. People responded well to Kathleen. However, on election night, as Kathleen's victory party was set up across the street from the courthouse at the Towson National Guard Armory, the votes heaped up for a convincing Bentley win: 94,404 votes to 66,943. Kathleen's husband, three daughters, mother, parents-in-law, cousin Patrick and uncle Ted were there to support her in her defeat. How did she deal with failure? Clearly, this is a term that Kathleen cannot accept. She bristles:

> I don't see it as a failure. . . . I mean, I lost a campaign. What I was really taught when growing up was that if I fell off my horse, I got back on and kept going. I think I ran a great campaign. I was running against an incumbent. It's not much fun to lose. Would I rather have won? Of course.

Why did she lose? Some say that her strong stand on insisting that the draft be reinstated, and that women be sent into combat hurt her a great deal. Among her mentors was Congresswoman Pat Schroeder (D-Colo), who had said, "Try it. If it doesn't work, then it doesn't work."

Worthwhile Work

Kathleen had gone into combat in Baltimore, and it didn't work. So, instead of heading down Route 95 to Washington each day for a session of Congress, she drops her kids off at school and then heads for her office in downtown Baltimore where she is director of a state educational program called the Maryland Student Service Alliance (MSSA).

Above her desk in her cluttered government-style cubicle is a print of an Andrew Wyeth austere barn. Close by is a colorful child's drawing. Handpainted posters outside in the hallway carry sentiments that she believes in from Andy Warhol, Billie Holiday, Margaret Mead, and others: "In the future, everyone will have fifteen minutes of fame" (Warhol); "Them that gots gets" (Holiday); and, "Never doubt that a small group of thoughtful, committed citizens can change the world" (Mead).

Kathleen has never been interested in fashion. She wears what is appropriate. No frills, no fuss. Today it's a businesslike black suit (the jacket is forgotten—crumpled on the seat under her), black and white polka dot blouse, a gold cross on a gold chain, and a swatch watch. Her straight brown hair, flecked with a little grey, is cut severely at the chin. She wears neither makeup nor pretension.

Kathleen Townsend is a workaholic. Her vacation at Hyannis Port this summer was merely a respite between a working trip to the Soviet Union and her work in Baltimore. And even then she found herself working, not sunbathing.

Her work is carrying out a 1985 mandate written into the State Board of Education's bylaws that requires every high school to introduce some form of public service into the curriculum. In the fall of 1987, when she called the board's head, David Hornbeck, not one school had initiated such a program. Kathleen saw this both as a serious omission and a great opportunity. Talking to Hornbeck, she stressed her personal commitment to public service, and asked that she be given a chance to put some teeth into the law. Hornbeck agreed, and in

January 1988, her office opened with no staff, just Kathleen.

She immersed—even impaled—herself into the program. It had all the qualities of a "good Kennedy program"—looking like a potential win-win situation for all involved. High schoolers could volunteer to work in soup kitchens and old-age homes, hopefully doing good, and building their self-esteem and receiving academic credit at the same time. Among the program's other aims are to help break down stereotypical barriers. As Kathleen describes it, "Our effort is to bring children from different backgrounds—black/white, rich/poor, public/private schools, et cetera, together." And while she facilitates this, Kathleen can earn some recognition in this town for her next political bout.

Money, of course, is not her motive for doing this job. But then, being a Kennedy means that she doesn't need to worry about that. Kathleen is not embarrassed to admit it:

A lot of my brothers and sisters can make a lot more money too. . . . They understand that you do get some satisfaction by trying to make a difference. The crowning joy of life is public service. And I think that's really a strong part of my family and there's a great deal of satisfaction in that. Thomas Jefferson wrote about life, liberty, and the pursuit of happiness. If you read Hannah Arendt, she talks about what he (Jefferson) means by happiness . . . in her book on revolution, and of course I go along with her on this—she says that what he was referring to was the happiness of participating in public affairs. I think this is what we should teach children as well.

A Weakness for Chocolate

It's hard not to like this Kennedy. She is candid and persuasive, has a sense of humor, and does not take herself overly seriously, despite her obvious intelligence. Her instincts are those of a politician, though. She knows when to react, and to whom, and her sense of timing is uncanny. When she doesn't like a question she rolls her eyes at a third person in the office as if to say, "What a silly question, don't you agree?"

She is also a feminist, though without the negative trappings. "I don't think I would have ever got really involved 'in politics' or gone to law school if it hadn't been for the feminist movement," she says. Yet, a superwoman of the eighties, she has struck a successful balance between family and career, managing to give her all to both:

> It's important that I care for my children—that's an important function of my marriage—and at the same time that I can go on and make a contribution (to society). I can combine the two—it's difficult, but it is possible. I just do it at different times. There were times when I didn't work, times that I worked part-time, and times that I worked full-time. That kind of flexibility is wonderful for Kathleen Kennedy Townsend, who obviously has some means, but it would be important that society provide those opportunities for lots of women so they don't feel that they're stuck.

She talks about the maternity leave bill that was recently struck down in Congress, aghast that the government is so apparently insensitive to the concerns of working mothers. She feels that the matter of requiring a paid minimum maternity leave is something that should not be left up to employers.

In her mother's day, the role of women in that patriarchal family was clearly defined. Wives were to support their husbands and raise their children, not to run for elective office themselves. That role was reserved for men. Today, Kathleen has dealt with this, though: "Clearly people have grown accustomed (to the notion) that men are the ones to run. . . . It's the way of life." Then a wistful reflection: "I think Eunice would have been a great elected official; and so would my grandmother Rose. . . ." She shrugs her shoulders—they couldn't, but she still has a chance.

When talking to Kathleen, one remembers that she is the oldest child of Robert Kennedy—often dubbed the most Kennedy of the Kennedys. She embodies her father's competitiveness and loyalty. When asked about the positive aspects of growing up as a Kennedy, she says, "It raises expectations, is a source of pride, and makes me feel fortunate." She will not list any negatives however, saying, "I don't pay any attention (to them)." Regarding her personal strengths, she mentions not giving up and trying her best to get a job done. On the other hand, when pushed to reveal a few of her weaknesses, she refers to an incident in which her mother was asked to list Kathleen's strengths and weaknesses. Ethel gladly elaborated on her many strengths, but the only weakness she identified was "chocolate."

Kathleen has strong views about many things, some of which she has begun to voice in several publications. The education of children is one of her priorities. In the January 1990 issue of *Washington Monthly* she has a piece called "Not just Read and Write, But Right and Wrong." In it she quotes from the conclusion of a study conducted by a liberal lobbying organization, People for the American Way: "Young people . . . reveal notions of America's unique character that emphasize freedom and license almost to the complete exclusion of service or participation. . . ." Kathleen says that schools should be taking responsibility to teach children values.

Community work is a major thrust of MSSA during the summer months. The rest of the year, students work within their own schools. One success story involved Suitland High School, outside of Washington. A severe absenteeism rate was corrected by simply forming a telephone chain to make wake-up calls. It resulted in an 87 percent improved attendance rate.

Despite significant accomplishments, MSSA has a way to go. It has grown from zero involvement three years ago to forty-five schools and more than 1,500 students today, and has gained recognition as a model for the country. But there are still 195 high schools in the state that continue to ignore the state's mandate. "It's a lesson in bureaucracy," says Kathleen's assistant, Maggie O'Neill. "To get to the teachers, we have to go through a central system. And there are only two of us." This year the program received government funding for the first time—$150,000 for the fiscal year of 1990. "It's not enough," Maggie says, "but it helps."

At the end of the day, Kathleen usually returns to her seventy-year-old white frame house in Ruxton, a suburb of Baltimore, where she lives with her husband and their three daughters: Meaghan, 12, Maeve, 10, and Kate, 6. David is an associate professor of classics and French literature at St. John's College in Annapolis. "When I can be home, I prefer to be with my children," she says, so she keeps her social engagements limited. "I've been out to dinner just for pleasure about four times in four years," she explains. Her evenings are usually spent helping them with homework, playing games, and discussing world events. Reading bible stories every night and quizzing their children on history at the dinner table are part of the Townsends' routine, echoing the Kennedy family tradition:

We have maps of Saudi Arabia and Kuwait in the dining room and when we were explaining the recent Middle East crisis, they said "Oh, it's just like Risk." Clearly we want them to know what's going on. We try to teach them to think on all kinds of levels. It's really very similar to what I did when growing up. So many kids don't know that they can make a difference. You've got to teach them.

Participation in sports is also urged in the Kennedy-Townsend family. The two older children ski, play tennis, and swim. Maeve, the only girl on a local soccer team, holds her own with the boys. Meaghan also enjoys gymnastics.

Although their household of pets is ordinary compared to the exotic animals Kathleen grew up with (including a sea lion called Sandy, who made the swimming pool his home), the Kennedy-Townsends also house a menagerie—a golden retriever, umpteen cats, a snake (which sometimes gets loose), goldfish, and hamsters. "We used to have rabbits too, but I ended up cleaning the cages out all the time," Kathleen says.

Born on the Fourth of July

Born on Independence Day in 1951, Kathleen Hartington Kennedy has spent her life fighting for her own independence. She was named after her father's sister, the Marchioness of Hartington, who died in a plane crash in 1948—just one of a string of tragedies in the Kennedy family that would eventually involve an entire nation. However, Robert Kennedy placed a condition on the naming of his first child—that she never be called "Kick," his sister's nickname. He had revered his fun-loving, strong-willed sister until she defied their father and married an Englishman outside her Catholic faith.

He did not want his daughter to follow the same rebellious course.

During the sixties, Kathleen gave her father plenty of occasion to worry as she pursued her own personal revolution. Yet unlike her aunt, she stayed within the bounds of family acceptance. She questioned her Catholicism—convincing her father to allow her to attend the non-Catholic co-ed Putney School in Vermont—but never abandoned it.

As the eldest, Kathleen had no contemporary cousins. She was followed by three brothers, and her first sister wasn't born until she was five. Thus, it fell to her to lead the others, not simply to be their pal. She was also given authority to dole out punishment to her siblings when necessary. Whether they were actually that good or whether she was overly lenient, she didn't have to discipline them often.

In various biographies written about the Kennedys, her siblings apparently considered Kathleen the smartest, the one with the strongest will to succeed, and the most religious. Yet she rebelled against the restraints of Catholicism during her high school years, protesting that she wanted to experience a wider outlook on life. She even stopped going to mass regularly, which hurt her mother deeply. When asked recently about her religiosity today, she tersely replies, "I go to mass." She believes that the Catholic Church is progressing, although not quickly enough.

Yet the bible, if not the Catholic Church, means a great deal to Kathleen. As a girl, she found wisdom and understanding there, and was the first of the cousins to comprehend the meaning of her grandmother's favorite saying, "To whom much has been given, much will be required," a quote from Saint Luke.

Kathleen certainly was given much—and not just materially. She inherited qualities of character from both her parents—a direct, unassuming nature and impatience with trivialities from her father and a vivacious, energetic disposition from her mother. On the other hand, she tended to be disorderly, displaying a lack of interest in her appearance. She did, however, observe old-fashioned courtesies, such as standing up when an elder entered the room, like all the Kennedy children.

Unlike some of her cousins, Kathleen understood early that her family was affluent. But she didn't realize the extent of her family's wealth until brought face to face with others who were starving. During a 1966 family vacation on a white-water raft expedition down the Colorado River, her naiveté was abandoned when her father added a visit to an American Indian reservation to the itinerary. "It was such a shock to be there for reasons of pleasure, and then to see the awful contrast —the way people on the reservation lived," Kathleen said. "I assume most wealthy people never see that part of life. That's why they're not moved to do something."

The ambience of Hickory Hill was somewhat like living out the rhyme, "There was an old woman, who lived in a shoe, she had so many children. . . ." Kids and animals were everywhere. And the extremes to which the family took its friendly competition in games and playful pranks were often egged on by mom or dad.

After her uncle was elected president in 1960, her father became his attorney general, head of the Justice Department, and a member of his cabinet. Politicians, journalists, and intellectuals soon became regular visitors to the house.

Kathleen was twelve when her uncle Jack was assassinated. Her father withdrew from the Justice Department, and, for a time, from life. In 1964, he decided to run for the U.S. Senate from New York, and won easily. Once again, politicians, journalists, and intellectuals filled the McLean mansion.

Kathleen's years at the Putney School were mind-expanding. She studied alongside children of farmers, blue-collar workers, teachers, and writers, and discovered the freedom of being able to think for herself, distanced from the Catholic way and her family's way. During this time, her father challenged Lyndon B. Johnson for the Democratic Party nomination for the presidency. The family's excitement over their possible return to the White House, though, was abruptly shattered. Kathleen's deepest fear since the assassination of her uncle had become a reality.

Awakened from a peaceful sleep in her dorm, she learned that her father had been shot. She flew to Los Angeles the next morning and just managed to see RFK before he died. Sixteen years old, she kept her grief private, and determined to continue her father's important work rather than to wallow in anger and self-pity. She knew that, among her brothers and sisters, she was fortunate. At least she had her father throughout her childhood. Her younger brothers and sisters would have to grow up without him.

The horror of that night changed Kathleen. She would customarily balance her serious side with a kind of mischievousness that she often acted upon. But from then on, the sober-minded, intense side of her personality prevailed.

Both to escape public attention and to fulfill a promise she had made to herself and to her father, Kathleen spent the following summer working with a Navajo tribe in Arizona. This experience, and a profound desire to live out her father's dream, led her in the direction of public service.

She determined to attend Radcliffe College and continue in the footsteps of her father and uncles. One summer during her college years, while backpacking through Europe with a friend, Kathleen decided to visit her paternal grandmother, Rose Kennedy, now 100, who was staying at the Maurice in Paris. The sight of her eldest granddaughter, wearing jeans, a floppy hat, a backpack and long flowing unkempt hair shocked the wealthy matron. If as Kathleen's appearance professed, she was so deeply offended by "the system," why not give away her inheritance, Rose wanted to know? Kathleen said that she would give the idea some thought. But that was as far as she went.

The highlight of Kathleen's Radcliffe years was meeting David Townsend, her red-bearded tutor, six feet four inches tall and four years her senior, with whom she studied southern United States literature during her sophomore year. They shared an interest in ecology, were both intent upon living simply, and were raised Catholic. In 1972 Kathleen and David planned a three-week trip down the Mississippi River on a raft called the Snopes, to honor Mark Twain's Huckleberry Finn. The trip proved to be more of an adventure than they had expected—David ended up with a hairline skull fracture. (Kathleen surprised herself when, angered after a two-hour wait, she resorted to using her family name at the hospital to get David treated.) Nonetheless, the experience bonded them, and the following September they became engaged. The wedding took place on November 17, 1973, at Holy Trinity Church in Washington. Uncle Ted gave his brother's daughter away. Ironically, the senator's eldest son, Ted Jr., had his leg amputated the same day.

After Kathleen graduated from Radcliffe, David took a job teaching English at St. John's College in Santa Fe, New Mexico, a branch of the Annapolis school. Kathleen entered law school at the University of New Mexico, but took a leave of absence after their first daughter was born. David switched to law, too, and the Townsends moved to New Haven, Connecticut, where they both attended Yale. Their second daughter was born soon after Kathleen received her law degree. Following David's graduation, the family moved to Ruxton.

The Townsends are, by all accounts, one of the best

matched couples of their time. Their three daughters were all delivered by natural childbirth at home, one of them by David alone. The Kennedy clan still gathers at Hickory Hill on holidays, and at Hyannis Port in the summer, and the new generation is forming friendships: "My daughter Maeve and 'my brother' Joe's children are very good friends and go fishing together," Kathleen says. "My daughter Kate is best friends with Kyle, Michael's child. When I went away for a couple of days she stayed with him."

Other wealthy families can enjoy their wealth, content to restrict their concern for their fellow men to making monetary donations a few times a year. Why is so much expected of the Kennedys?

Compared to most people, we really are lucky. People have very tough lives. I came from a great family. I work with kids all the time who have lousy lives. They're beaten, their parents don't speak English, they don't have a father at home. Look how fortunate I've been. Obviously I'm not going to say "woe is me." I really do think that caring for others is important, and it's clearly easier if you have the means. We *should* be able to do it, to achieve whatever task is at hand.

And she probably will.

Joseph P. Kennedy II
Heir to the Throne

A grueling session of Congress is behind him and another rigorous yet imminently successful campaign is ahead. It's August 1990 and Joe Kennedy is "off-schedule," as his assistant has no doubt been instructed to term his vacation.

Joe will not have much time to relax, however, with a primary looming on September 18. But this campaign will be much easier than the first and less tense than the second, as he has proven himself to be a valuable asset to the people of the Eighth Congressional District of Massachusetts. After all, he is the incumbent, and more importantly, a Democrat. A Republican has never held the seat in the history of this district. The most devastating obstacle to anyone running against him, though, is that his last name is Kennedy. Many people in the district still have fond memories of his Uncle Jack, kissing their babies and shaking their hands, from the time when he, too, was their congressman. There is even a shared feeling of responsibility for JFK's ultimate success since it was here where he began. A shoo-in? Of course, but publicly Joe says that he prefers to wait until the votes come in.

A point, frustrating to feminists, is that Joseph P. Kennedy II, the first grandson of the family's patriarch, Joseph Patrick Kennedy I, has often been referred to as the heir to the intangible throne, even though his politically active older sister, Kathleen, was in fact the first grand*child*. Still, even in these days and times, Joe wears the crown as the eldest male. After all, that's how it works in royal families.

The Apple Closest to the Tree

Born on September 24, 1952, to Robert and Ethel, Joe came into the world with both a crown on his head and the proverbial silver spoon in his mouth. Joe receives an annual income from his trust fund, worth somewhere between $300,000 and $400,000. The ultimate worth of the entire family fortune remains a mystery, even to many members of the family.

Joe once said in an interview for a book on his first congressional campaign, *A Race for the Eighth,* "I hate the word 'legacy.' There's a tremendous inclination out there to think that somehow I feel some crazy obligation to pick up—what would it be—the torch." But he cannot ignore the fact that after three generations of public service, the Kennedy name itself causes many of the family, as well as the public, to expect him, as the eldest male of his generation, to pick up that torch. People hope that he will carry on in the tradition of what the Kennedy name has come to mean to millions all over the world. He should appreciate the obvious, that to those who were expecting it, announcing his candidacy for Congress was picking up that torch. And if Joe has his way, it will again burn brightly in the eyes of the American public.

Joe, with his dark blond curls, football lineman build and overall rugged looks, is not the spitting image of his father. Yet in spirit, he is similar. He has the same passion for helping the needy, the same impatience (except with children), and the same unyielding mindset and energy for getting the job done. Appearance aside, he bears a striking resemblance to the man he has mentioned as his primary political idol—his father.

Every Kennedy is physically "Kennedyesque" in some way, however, and for Joe, the indelible stamp is his wide toothy grin, broad jawline, and deep-set eyes.

Growing up in northern Virginia, a noticeable missing element is his lack of the famous Cape Cod accent.

The dissimilarity that Joe is most sensitive about is his reputation for *not* being bookishly bright. Unlike famous Kennedys before him, studying never held his interest. Although he adhered to the strict demands that were placed on every Kennedy child: dutifully writing research papers on public figures every Sunday, participating in educational conversations during meals, taking oral quizzes given by his mom on the ride to school, and reading at least one hour a day (comic books not allowed), schoolwork to him was an unnecessary drill. Joe was later diagnosed as dyslexic, which might explain his difficulty as a student.

This young Kennedy learned how to get by in spite of his dyslexia. He put enough effort into his schoolwork to get by—but just barely. Jumping from one private school to another and eventually from one college to another, Joe finally landed a degree in 1976 from the less-than-elite University of Massachusetts in Boston.

Whatever training Joe avoided in school was compensated for, however, by the political training he received growing up in the stimulating Kennedy environment. Just consider the quality of his teachers! His cousin Chris Lawford once said, "We were all, every one of us, raised to be president." Joe, in particular, was groomed early, just as his Uncle Joe, and Uncle Jack before him. Joe's parents tried to infuse him with political desire. His greatest training would have been working on his dad's presidential campaign in 1968. Joe still remembers the massive excitement he felt when his father promised that he could work with him full time—just weeks before Bobby was murdered.

Earlier than most, Joe also learned the meaning of responsibility. After the shock of his Uncle Jack's death, Joe received a note from his dad:

On the day of the burial of your Godfather John Fitzgerald Kennedy

THE WHITE HOUSE

November 24, 1963

Dear Joe,

You are the eldest of the male grandchildren. You have a special and particular responsibility now which I know you will fulfill.

Remember all the things that Jack started—be kind to others that are less fortunate than we—and love our country.

Love to you,
Daddy

When the nation lost its president, eleven-year-old Joe lost the godfather and uncle he dearly revered. And just five years later, another brutal assassination of a Kennedy left Joe without a father.

Joe was asleep in his small room at Milton Academy when someone abruptly threw on the lights. Confused and groggy, Joe's eyes focused on Richard Clasby, a Harvard classmate of his Uncle Ted. He knew immediately that something must be desperately wrong. The news was the worst possible . . . his father had been shot in Los Angeles. Shocked by the reality of each piercing word, he did not cry. But the look of hurt and fear on his face is something Clasby says he will never forget. "Do you think he has a chance?" Joe kept asking, somehow sensing the answer.

Joe was able to get to his father's side a few hours before he died. He prayed, though with little hope, for this nightmare to turn around.

Americans sobbed as little John-John saluted the coffin of his father, JFK. But few realized the depth of quiet suffering Joe experienced when his father was killed. Unlike his young cousins, he was old enough to know the value of what he, his family, and the rest of the country had lost.

Joe had "IT"

Joe came through as a true Kennedy on the funeral train from New York to Washington, shaking every hand and saying, "Hi, I'm Joe Kennedy. Thanks a lot for coming." It was then, in the midst of grief, that people—especially his mother—started noticing that Joe had "IT": that Kennedy charm, strength and intangible something that even movie stars' agents can't put into words.

Always the leader of the pack of twenty-nine cousins at family gatherings at Hyannis Port and Hickory Hill, Joe suddenly became the male head of his family. This was silently symbolized when his mother seated him at his father's chair at the dinner table.

Striving to live up to the responsibility—and the legacy—Joe's emotional wounds sometimes got in the way. Unfortunately, his mother and Uncle Ted, his surrogate father, were too busy dealing with many other problems to help him. Joe managed to escape the temptation of drugs, which haunted the lives of two of his younger brothers, but he, too, struggled through adolescence. He described the next ten years of his own life as "being in limbo."

The press, on the other hand, often lampooned his escapades during those years in an unflattering manner. This personal introduction to the world of reporters began a lifelong obsession with keeping his private life as secret as possible. The only black mark on Joe's record was a conviction for negligence he received for driving a car that was involved in a serious accident. Swerving to miss an oncoming car, his car flipped, ejecting its seven occupants and then smashing into a tree. Joe and three of the passengers escaped serious injury. But two girls were very badly hurt and his brother David suffered a bad back injury. One of the girls, Pamela Kelley, was paralyzed for life from the waist down and received a $1 million settlement. Joe still keeps in contact with her out of a sense of friendship and responsibility. The accident finally sobered him out of adolescent carelessness and selfishness, and into the responsibilities of adulthood.

Many Kennedy cousins have gone through the sort of rebellious, adventurous, and uncertain period common to American youth. Joe's rite of passage occurred when his Uncle Ted asked him to manage his 1976 Senate campaign. After a successful race, Joe said that he liked the taste of politics but inside felt a need to do something to prove himself before thinking about running for office. Many critics expected that Joe Kennedy would just go out and run on his name alone—but he wanted to run on more, to achieve something first.

His father's vigilance over the plight of America's poor and less fortunate was becoming Joe's concern as well. At a ceremony dedicating the John F. Kennedy Presidential Library in 1979, Joe summarized his feelings tersely. "My father died waging a struggle. As I have grown up, I've come to appreciate what that struggle was about."

His concern for the impoverished began to focus on their inability to sufficiently heat their homes during winter. Joe created a nonprofit company, Citizens Energy Corporation, which became his own personal contribution and eventual stepping-stone into politics. "Families now face a choice between heating and eating, and that is a completely unacceptable choice for our government to provide," Joe stated as he announced the formation of Citizens Energy in 1979. "We're taking all the profits normally made on sales and funneling them back to lower fuel costs," he explained. Started on a shoestring (of some mighty big shoes), Citizens Energy now grosses $1.5 billion a year. Joe's brother Michael took over as chairman of the company in 1986.

Having created something to provide a personal sense of identity while making it known that he had made a commitment to the plight of the underprivileged, Joe was ready. He would miss the fascination of big business, but felt that it was a good time to enter the alluring world of politics.

First attracted to the lieutenant governorship of Massachusetts, Joe was surprised that he did not receive the kind of support he expected. This was not so much because he was a poor choice, but because he was too good. Advisors to Governor Michael Dukakis were apparently concerned about being upstaged by a Kennedy, so he decided not to push his political ambitions into such unreceptive waters.

Unscathed, he considered a run for Congress. The legendary Tip O'Neill, Speaker of the House, had decided to retire, which left his (and Joe's) 8th District seat open. On December 5, after consulting his political advisers, his mother and his wife, Joe announced his candidacy.

He ran on a platform of human rights and living necessities for the working class: food, energy, housing, health care, and education, always popular concerns in this liberal, Democratic, working-class district. But whatever his stand on the issues, his name, with its financial power and nostalgic ring, was the key. George Bachrach, one of his opponents in the Democratic primary, surmised that Joe Kennedy would only have to *earn* 16 percent of the vote, since his name would provide the other 35 percent.

But Joe did not want to depend on speculation. He worked very hard and spent an enormous amount of money—an announced $1,550,916. Spending money became a necessity for the other candidates when a Kennedy entered the race. The sixteen original candidates spent over $3.8 million, making it the most expensive congressional race ever. They knew that once Joe Kennedy entered the game, he would fight hard to the finish, with winning his only goal.

Political Washington chuckled when Joe drew one of the lowest numbers in the congressional office lottery as a first-term congressman, and wound up with one of the smallest, out-of-the-way offices on Capitol Hill. It relieved some of the other freshmen's jealousy over the attention Joe was getting. Unabashed, Joe surrounded himself with family photographs and his children's artwork, giving his office a personal and comfortable feeling, then headed out onto the floor of Congress.

Although aggressive by nature, Joe has played the role of a newcomer to Congress relatively well, during his first and second terms, receiving only one reported tongue-thrashing from his Uncle Ted. He violated protocol by speaking out of turn and in a raised voice to a senior senator. "Don't you *ever* talk to Sam Nunn like that!" his uncle warned. The uncle in the Senate and the nephew in the House were seeking support of the powerful senator from Georgia for an amendment to set hiring goals for Catholics at a major U.S. firm in Ireland. Nunn's strong, uncompromising resistance sparked Joe's temper. (The Kennedys won anyway—the amendment was approved.)

Though Joe's tactics do not always work, he rationalizes, "If you are going to make some enemies because you did the right thing, that's what life is all about."

Joe is carrying on the Kennedy tradition of running a well-staffed office providing excellent constituent services. He serves on the House Committee on Banking, Finance, and Urban Affairs; the House Committee on Veterans Affairs; and the Select Committee on Aging. The following is a partial list of his accomplishments:

• Obtaining a visa for a stranded Lebanese baby adopted by a couple in his district.

• Withdrawal of a government request to close down an Army laboratory that employed his constituents.

• Saving $85 million in funding to aid the homeless.

• Filing the Veterans' Nurse Pay Act to upgrade the VA nurses' pay scale.

• Pushing for and winning a major antidiscrimination measure in the savings and loan bailout bill, which required lending institutions to disclose lending patterns.

Plans to Stay Awhile

In lieu of other options always open to a Kennedy, his current desire is to stay where he is and emerge as a leader in Congress. "I'd like to make a career out of being a congressman," he stated. Joe has gained the respect of his peers and even a few of the old guard for his persistence and willingness to do his homework.

Joe launched his 1990 reelection campaign with the statement, "I intend to seek reelection to the United States Congress and to continue my work on affordable housing, antidiscrimination, human rights and protecting the interests of working people and the poor."

One thing is certain—he's not in this for the salary. He has explained that he doesn't need the money. Kennedys are able to spend time on public concerns, without having to worry about how to put food on their own tables. Yet Joe has at times revealed that his privilege has bred insensitivity toward the very people whose plight he seeks to champion. "People are more interested in their jobs than in poverty," he once said, after leaving an agency administering programs for the poor.

Realistically, people who don't protect their jobs will, with their families, become part of the poverty problem. A young Kennedy can mouth off at Sam Nunn, or even lose a reelection, but not John or Jane Doe. Most non-Kennedys lack the security of a trust fund and the embrace of a powerful and protective family, so they don't risk losing their jobs by speaking their minds to their boss.

But Joe is still a shining young knight to some, and even a hero to others. Mildred Akaka, in particular, may even owe her life to Joe. In July 1990, while out in a charter boat in a fishing tournament, the young Congressman heard a distress call. Joe and two crew members jumped into the water and rescued a young woman whose boat overturned during a struggle with a 485 pound marlin. Unknown to Joe, the waters were infested with sharks. Once Joe realized the danger they had both been in he first said, "It kind of nearly gave me heart failure," and then added, "It was classic *Old Man and the Sea* stuff." It turned out that the woman he rescued is the niece of one of Joe's Democratic political colleagues, Daniel Akaka, U.S. senator from Hawaii.

Though Joe has chosen a public life, he tries hard to control the public's access to him. Reportedly refusing 98 percent of interview requests, his passion for privacy is only surpassed by that of his famously elusive Aunt Jackie (Onassis). One is more likely to drown in the moat around his castle than to gain entrance. Savvy enough not to offend, members of his staff are the ones who hand out the "nos." The loyalty of his close friends is admirable. In fact, the trust that most Kennedys receive from their friends is a phenomenon. However, once the door is opened, the man himself is boisterous yet courteous, with a lot of charm and some tender spots. He has come a long way.

In 1980, with escapades of adolescent Kennedys intermittently surfacing in the news, Bill Adler recorded the opinion of a Kennedy family observer in a book, *The Kennedy Children.* "Once the fortune is established and the family becomes aristocratic, the blood line thins out. There aren't any more big money-makers among the Kennedys, no heavy movers. And pretty soon all that's left is a bunch of empty-headed playboys and playgirls, running around from discos to beaches to yachts. That's where the Kennedys are headed. . . ."

Joe turned his life around, and proved this Kennedy-watcher wrong. It's been ten years since the young Kennedys took to the discos. They've traded wild parties with the likes of Mick Jagger for less rebellious pursuits. Joe still loves his sailing and overall jet-setting, but has shown signs of understanding the satisfaction of a life that gives something back of what he has been so blessed to have.

Joe lists twin sons as his greatest two blessings. One of his favorite achievements on the Hill was to write a congressional resolution making October 8 National Children's Day. Joe explained how his sons inspired him: "It really came down to a little conversation between me and my boys a year or so ago, where they pointed out that there was a Mother's Day and a Father's Day, but lo and behold there was no Children's Day. And they thought that was kind of an outrage."

Joe often felt neglected as a child. His caring yet absent father was lost to him much too soon. His mother then needed Joe to grow up overnight, despite the urgency of his own wants and needs. He and his mother enjoy a good relationship now, but the earlier years were tough. With this experience in his privileged background and seeing the suffering of many of America's poor children, Joe has developed a special sensitivity to the needs of all children, rich or poor.

"It seems to me that if we aren't about, as a nation and as a people, building a better world for our youngsters, than we really have lost our way," he says.

Robert Kennedy once said that his most powerful emotions stemmed not from his position, power, or wealth but from his children. As the proud father of the eldest two males of the *next* generation of Kennedys, Joe now understands what his father meant. Joseph Patrick III and Matthew Rauch, born on October 4, 1980, are privileged children of a devoted, protective and loving father. Joe regrets that, after eleven years of marriage, he had to put them through the hardship of their parents' separation in March 1989, and divorce (filed in September 1990). But it was an inevitable outcome, since his wife severely disliked the public life that Joe was building in Washington. Joe met Sheila Brewster Rauch at Harvard where she received her baccalaureate and masters degrees. A debutante from a prominent Philadelphia family, she seemed an acceptable match for a Kennedy. An Episcopalian, she agreed to raise their children as Catholics. When they decided to separate after ten years, Sheila and the kids moved to Cambridge, and Joe stayed in their house in Brighton.

Their separation prompted Joe to withdraw from the gubernatorial race in 1990, announcing both the separation and withdrawal of his candidacy on the same day. He said, "As a father, my principal obligation and deepest personal desire is to assist my children through this most difficult time in their lives. I am dedicated to public service, but I love my children. This means that I intend to give a great deal of my time and energies to Matt and Joe." He did not feel that he would have the time to do both well.

Critics doubted the total sincerity of that statement. Though Joe was the Democratic front-runner, his withdrawal led to speculation that he mainly backed out because of a concern that the publicity surrounding his separation would cost him too many votes.

As a single parent in a world where the problems of the atomic family haunt even Kennedys, Joe seeks to maintain the difficult balance between a congressman's harried public life and the private needs of his precious two sons.

When asked about future goals, and more specifically his thoughts on running for president someday, Joe says, "People who make such game plans always end up disappointing themselves. . . ." A curious answer considering that his grandfather was the kingpin of game planning, and his family is known for its behind-the-scenes preparations.

At times, Joe's statements can border on the reckless. When asked how he would raise money for his social programs, Joe said, "I'll tax the rich."

However, this Joe is of another generation and a different mindset. He has received solid marks in his first four years as a congressman, far better than he did in school. Although his name may have helped him get to Washington, he is now graded on his performance.

Spiritually inspired, his political mantra is "Democracy, Opportunity, America," which he repeats to himself quite often. But when Joe is "off-schedule" or on personal time, he focuses on Joseph and Matthew. . . . the heirs to Joe Kennedy's throne.

Robert F. Kennedy Jr.

White Knight of the Environment

Earth Day 1990 was no one-time event for Robert F. Kennedy, Jr. In an era of environmental chic, when celebrities like Streep and Redford link their names with movements against agricultural chemicals and global warming, the protection of the natural world is his everyday job.

In certain circles in metropolitan New York, Bobby Kennedy is something of a white knight of the environmental crusade. For seven years he has worked as a lawyer for the Hudson River Fishermen's Association. Year by year, case by case, he has built a record that his clients, at least, find laudable. He has challenged governments and companies that pollute the Hudson River and Long Island Sound. He has won settlements that have provided funding for an environmental monitor—the Soundkeeper—to watch over the Sound. He has brought cases that would expand a citizen's right to have safe and clean rivers, harbors, and shorefronts, and free access to those resources.

"Obviously, he doesn't have to do this," said Terry Backer, the Soundkeeper. "But the guy is committed to the environment. He works himself to death. You can call him at nine o'clock at night and he's in that office."

His office is in a house in White Plains, New York, near Pace University, where he teaches and directs the law school's Environmental Law Clinic. It is a paper-strewn cell, crammed with file cabinets and decorated with pictures of hawks and falcons. In a nearby bathroom—which had the only available blank wall—he has assembled a pastiche of topographical maps delineating the entire thirteen thousand square-mile watershed of the Hudson. A licensed wildlife rehabilitator, he has been known to keep injured animals in a small cage outside the front door so he could feed them throughout the day: on one occasion, for example, he regularly interrupted his work to thrust lumps of cat food down the gullet of an abandoned, unfledged crow. Inside, he meets with students at what would otherwise be the dining room table. He supervises eight graduate environmental law students at the clinic who put in twenty-four hours a week in pursuit of polluters. "They learn how to practice law and they learn how to be good environmentalists," he said, "and at the same time we get the river cleaned up."

If this public service is a legacy bequeathed on the younger generation of Kennedys, RFK Jr., at least, does not find it onerous.

"I don't regard it as a sacrifice," he said. "I regard it as something that's fulfilling to me and I'm lucky to do it. The idea came from my grandfather, who had a notion that this country has been very good to the Kennedys and we owed it something in return. It's something that has been passed down from my father's generation to us."

Born January 17, 1954, Bobby Kennedy is the third child of Senator Robert F. Kennedy Sr. He was educated at Harvard, received his law degree at the University of Virginia, and then in 1987 became the first person to earn a master's degree in environmental law from Pace University, in White Plains, New York.

But to call him merely an environmental lawyer can be misleading: Environmental lawyers come in at least two versions.

One represents corporations or real estate developers, helping them, as often as not, to prepare environmental impact statements that meet the letter of the law but obfuscate real effects on the environment; guiding them through regulations so they can provide just as much environmental protection as is necessary and no more. Hired guns, their purpose is to see that environmental laws do not hinder their clients' business.

The other represents the public, either through citizens groups or non-profit organizations, and has the difficult but often fruitful job of clearing up the obfuscations and latching on to the maneuverings of the corporate and real estate lawyers. Well-trained academically and experienced in legal practice, they are often people whose commitment to the environment derives from a passion for the natural world.

Bobby Kennedy Jr. fits into the second category. He brings to the law an outdoorsman's knowledge of natural history, gained through years of studying birds, hiking, diving, rafting, and observing wildlife in North America, South America, and Africa.

"I always was interested in conservation and the environment. Since I was born I was interested in animals," Kennedy said.

It was an interest that was tolerated and encouraged by his parents. As a boy he collected snakes and lizards. For his thirteenth birthday, his father had a naturalist from the Bronx Zoo construct a walk-in terrarium, stocked with seventy-five species of animals. He grew fond of falcons and falconry, feeding live pigeons to the fierce, captive raptors. Falcons are skilled at taking birds on the wing—as small as sparrows or as big as ducks—and young Bobby would let them snare homing pigeons. When his father expressed unease at seeing pigeons used as live food, the two Kennedys reached an agreement. If a pigeon was quick enough and skilled enough to dodge a falcon twice in a row, it was considered spared and never was forced again to take on the formidable predators. As a teenager in Hyannis, Massachusetts, Bobby often could be seen—menacingly, one would imagine—posed with a hawk gripping his gloved hand. Also as a teenager he visited the Serengeti in Africa to watch and photograph animals, saying all along that his fondest goal was to become a veterinarian.

After college, Bobby Kennedy worked for the Manhattan district attorney and then hitched on with the Hudson River Fishermen's Association, as a volunteer at first. Among those in the younger generation of Kennedys, he had been the one who was considered ideal for politics. Tall, handsome, with an unmistakable Kennedy demeanor, he was talked about openly as being presidential material or "like Jack." He seemed to be of two minds about his own celebrity. Published accounts describe triumphal visits to Haiti and Alabama, where his reception was almost messianic. But in those same accounts he remembers wistfully the time, for example, when as a teenager he escaped to the West Coast and spent his days "riding around with bums. It was good: I could be one of them and not be a Kennedy."

"People are always judging me as my father's son," he has said. "Someone always seems to notice me. Someone is always scrutinizing me."

With the Hudson River Fishermen's Association he sought and received anonymity.

In 1986 he prepared lawsuits for the group against Norwalk, Bridgeport and Stratford, Connecticut, for dumping sewage into Long Island Sound in violation of the Clean Water Act. Among those at a press conference called to announce the suits were Terry Backer, the burly and voluble Norwalk oysterman who would later become the Soundkeeper, and John Cronin, the Hudson Riverkeeper who is skilled at the impassioned rhetoric that escalates the public relations battles in the environmental war. But nobody that day mentioned the attorney who did the legal work. None of the reporters realized it was Bobby Kennedy.

The next year *The New Yorker* magazine published a profile of John Cronin, mentioning in one passage that the fishermen's association had an attorney who liked to scuba dive in the Hudson River and catch unusual specimens of fish, which he would preserve in the association's freezer. The profile referred to him simply as "the attorney" and did not mention his name.

In 1982, Bobby Kennedy married Emily Black. They settled in Bedford, a well-off community in the green exurbs of Westchester County, north of New York City, where they live with their two children, Bobby, who is six, and Kick, who is two. He shunned publicity, perhaps with good reason, for any event or transgression that became public found its way into the local newspaper—the birth of his first child, for example, or a speeding ticket that was noted on a police blotter.

By late 1988 he was making a tentative return to public life, but on his own terms. Speaking to a group about environmental issues on one occasion, he rebuffed a question about his family with a curt, "I don't talk about that."

At about the same time, those he worked with at the Hudson River Fishermen's Association and the Natural Resources Defense Council (where he is a project attorney) began to mention him publicly, credited him with successfully carrying out their campaign to turn the Hudson River and Long Island Sound back into healthy estuaries.

Through the years Bobby Kennedy has retained his interest in falconry. He is president of the New York Falconry Association. He owns a Harris hawk, which he works in the woods behind his house. He will free the bird, watch it rise to a perch atop a tree, and then walk quickly among the trees, his dog ranging ahead, scaring up small game. Catching rodents is no easy feat for the hawk, Kennedy said, and most forays end unsuccessfully. But the pleasure for him is not the kill but the hunt.

In his pursuit of those who break environmental laws, his attitude is the opposite. He goes for the kill, or at least the surrender in the form of a negotiated settlement. He will take a victory on the merits but is not shy about winning on technicalities. He is no radical—he campaigns locally for Democratic candidates—and he believes, generally, that existing laws are adequate (an exception: he has said in speeches that cars should be required to get at least forty miles per gallon). The problem, in his view, is that government regulators let other branches of government ignore environmental laws.

"They're not enforced," he said, "and you can see that in New York City. If New York City were forced to obey the law, Long Island Sound would be clean."

Bobby Kennedy's most frequent target as an environmental lawyer is government.

"He's a pioneer as an attorney in the area of municipal and governmental responsibility for environmental problems," said John Cronin. While it may be typical to hold industry accountable for the fate of the earth, Cronin credits Kennedy with espousing the principle that "all levels of government have gotten a free ride for many years regarding their direct pollution and environmental abuse activities."

Robert Funicello, a lawyer who was president of Federated Conservationists of Westchester County, an environmental group, said: "I think he's exactly what he appears to be—a serious young man, and to the environmental movement in Westchester County, extremely helpful and useful.

"He has a good sense of what the issues are and how to approach lawsuits. The way you're productive is recognizing important things and unimportant things, and going after the important things."

Funicello cited Kennedy's legal strategy in a suit against the Westchester County government brought early in 1990 by the Federated Conservationists, the fishermen's association, and a local environmentalist.

The instigation was an announcement by the county that budget constraints would force it to close several waterfront parks. These included Croton Point, a park leading to an area of the Hudson whose use for fishing has been documented back to eight thousand years ago. Kennedy's tack was to cite the public trust doctrine.

In New York, the doctrine holds that tidal lands are owned by the public and that the public may not be denied their use. Kennedy argued that the doctrine meant that the county government was obliged to keep its waterfront parks open, because if they were closed the public's access to the tidal areas would be cut off.

"The public trust doctrine didn't allow the county to close the parks," Kennedy said. "It was clear at Croton Point because it was used as a fishery since there were people on the continent."

"Although the point became moot when the county decided to keep the parks open—the threat of the suit probably was a factor—if the challenge had succeeded it would have greatly expanded the public trust doctrine by changing the definition of public trust lands to include not just tidal areas but public lands leading to them," Robert Funicello said. Kennedy further believes that, under the argument that the public is denied access to its public trust areas if they were closed because of pollution, the doctrine may be used potentially to force governments to clean up polluted waters.

Expanding the public trust doctrine was exactly what the lawsuit against Westchester County was meant to accomplish, Kennedy said: "Since the day I started working for the fishermen we've been trying to figure out how to use the public trust doctrine in a case. It has a lot of potential."

When Kennedy and the fishermen's association sue a branch of government, they are acting under a provision of the federal law which says in Kennedy's words,

"When government fails to act, citizens can step into the shoes of the United States attorney."

Thus shod, he has sued four municipalities in Connecticut—Greenwich, Stratford, Bridgeport, and Norwalk—for operating sewage treatment plants in violation of the Clean Water Act. The Greenwich and Bridgeport suits are still active. Norwalk and Stratford settled, for $150,000 and $200,000 respectively, plus guarantees that they will fix their sewage treatment plants. The guarantees include a schedule specifying certain dates by which improvements must be made, and penalties the municipalities must pay if the schedule is not met. It also includes penalties for violations other than those that prompted the suit, if they occur while improvements are being made. The settlement money funds the Soundkeeper and goes into local cleanup and management programs.

"We've probably sued more cities than any other environmental group in the country," Kennedy said.

In the Stratford suit, the son of a former Attorney General has been battling the United States Justice Department, which has been trying to claim $75,000 of the settlement under a provision of the law that allows the department to review settlements. Kennedy said the department's practice has been not only to review but to ask for half of the money. Having successfully battled one branch of government, groups often yield out of reluctance to fight another. The money, he said, fattens the United States Treasury and is not used for local projects.

"It goes to paint lines on highways, or mine harbors in Nicaragua, or whatever they do with it," he said. "It doesn't go back to Long Island Sound."

He added, "We're not going to give it to them."

In another suit, Kennedy and the fishermen's association succeeded in closing down the Remington Gun Club, which occupied a point of land on the Sound in

Stratford, at the mouth of the Housatonic River. Decades of target practice had filled the sediments with lead from shotgun shells. Tests showed that the sediments contained six hundred and forty thousand parts of lead per million; that is, almost two-thirds of the bottom of the Sound in that area were composed of a highly toxic heavy metal. Kennedy said that when he searched the records of federal Superfund sites, the largest concentration of lead he could find was about six thousand parts per million. He and the fishermen's association argued persuasively that shooting lead into the Sound in tiny increments from numerous guns over many years was no different than dumping it in via a large pipe.

"It's a novel application of the Clean Water Act to guns," said Kennedy. "The Clean Water Act basically is written so that it forbids discharges of pollutants from pipes into waterways. It's clear when you're dealing with a large pipe from an industrial facility that it's prohibited under that act. It's less clear to some people that little pipes—or guns—should be regulated. It's probably the most contaminated site in the country. Why that shouldn't be regulated is unclear to me."

The forays of the fishermen's association into Long Island Sound are recent compared to its work on the Hudson. Its members argue persuasively that the Sound, the Hudson, the East River, and New York Harbor are really one body of water made separate by political boundaries that have little to do with nature. It is currently involved in a suit against New York State, the immediate aim of which is to force the state to hold public hearings before giving New York City new permits for its fourteen sewage treatment plants. Its ultimate goal, Kennedy said, is to argue convincingly at those hearings that the city should be required to remove heavy metals from its treated sewage, as well as nitrogen, which has been linked to the severe loss of dissolved oxygen that afflicts the metropolitan area's waters in summer.

The philosophy behind Kennedy's willingness to use the courts is a simple one: "With the fishermen's association, it's ecosystem oriented, and we sue anybody who's going to hurt the Hudson," he said.

Kennedy and the fishermen's association are challenging a plan by New York City to siphon river water at its Chelsea pump station to supplement the city's supply of drinking water during droughts.

"The Chelsea case is probably one of the most creative cases we've been involved in with Bobby," said John Cronin, the Riverkeeper. "He was able to use an approach and an interpretation of the Clean Water Act in such a way that allowed us to go into federal court to protect the Hudson River fishery when New York City wanted to use the Hudson as an emergency source of water."

As Cronin explained it, the fishermen's association was afraid that if the city removed water from the Hudson it would throw off the balance between salt water and fresh that the river needs to survive as an estuary, which would threaten the river's spawning fish.

Kennedy saw that when the water was treated to make it fit to drink, two chemicals—chlorine and alum —ended up in the city's West Branch Reservoir, in Putnam County, north of Westchester, in violation of the Clean Water Act. He linked the direct pollution of the reservoir with the threat to the fish in the river. A federal judge agreed that there was a link and ordered the city to negotiate with the fishermen's association. As a result, the city agreed not to withdraw water in June and July, when newly-hatched fish are abundant and most vulnerable to changes in water chemistry.

"It put Chelsea into a new light, one that we had

Rose Fitzgerald Kennedy and Joseph Patrick Kennedy and their children, six of whom are the parents of the twenty-nine Kennedy cousins. Left to right: Eunice, Jack, Rosemary, Jean, Joseph, Teddy, Rose, Joe Jr., Patricia, Bobby, and Kathleen (Kick). (*John F. Kennedy Library*)

Robert F. Kennedy Jr., the environmental crusader.

RFK Jr. with his wife and children, Bobby and Kate, in front of their Mt. Kisco, New York home.

Congressman Joseph P. Kennedy II (D-Mass) at a reception. (*John F. Kennedy Library*)

Kerry, *right*, and sister Rory, *left*, present the 1987 Robert F. Kennedy Memorial Center's Human Rights Award to In Jae-Kun for her husband, a Korean political activist.

Only 21 years old, Patrick Kennedy was elected the state representative for the 9th Rhode Island district.

Patrick Kennedy and his mother, Joan, and well-wishers after his election victory in Providence, Rhode Island.

Since losing a leg to cancer, Edward Kennedy Jr. has become an ardent crusader for the civil rights of the mentally and physically handicapped. (*John F. Kennedy Library*)

Caroline Kennedy Schlossberg, reticent before reporters, is the author of a *New York Times* bestseller on the Constitution, *In Our Defense*.

John F. Kennedy Jr., the handsome hunk. (*John F. Kennedy Library*)

Maria Shriver Schwarzenegger, a television journalist for NBC, is married to world-famous body builder and actor Arnold Schwarzenegger.

Maria Shriver Schwarzenegger, with husband Arnold, attends a movie opening in New York with Jane Fonda *(AP/Wide World)*

The Smiths before their family was rocked by tragedy and scandal: *Left to right*, Steve Jr. (standing), Amanda, Steve Sr., Jean, Kym, and William (standing).
(Frank Teti Collection / John F. Kennedy Library)

William Kennedy Smith, acquitted of rape in a trial that shocked Palm Beach society and the nation. *(AP/Wide World)*

John F. Kennedy, Jr. and William Smith leave the Palm Beach County Courthouse during Smith's rape trial in 1991. *(AP/Wide World)*

A relaxed William Smith talks to his uncle, Sargent Shriver, during the trial. *(AP/Wide World)*

never before been able to find a forum for protecting the Hudson River fishery," said Cronin.

"It's very important," said Robert Boyle, the president of the fishermen's association and the author of books about the river, acid rain, and global warming. "We can all work like hell to clean up the Hudson River and in one fell swoop New York City can ruin the estuary by taking fresh water."

Having fought Kennedy numerous times, the city's Department of Environmental Protection takes the paradoxical view of him as both a "nuisance" and as someone who achieves goals the city wants to achieve but hasn't, said Ian Michaels, a spokesman for the department.

"Though we don't always agree with everything he does and don't always agree with the creative little lawsuits he comes up with against us, basically we're all working for the same thing," said Michaels. "We're all just trying to have enough clean water to go around. The lawsuits are something we have to live with."

Much of Bobby Kennedy's public emergence in Westchester County came via the lectern. By 1989 he was regularly making speeches to environmental groups, schools, political clubs, and just about any other organization that asked him. He charges no fee for local groups but if an honorarium is offered, he asks that it be given to the fishermen's association. (He is also on the national lecture circuit, and says it is the source of most of his income.) Those seeking a clear expression of the issues that concern him as a public figure can do no better than to attend one of his talks.

The basic Bobby Kennedy speech is a learned ramble, happily interdisciplinary in an era of specialization. It encompasses the globe and focuses on the Hudson River. He proffers a view of the United States as a nation gone astray from its historical link to the natural world and whose salvation lies in making that link again.

Referring to the environmental holocaust in Eastern Europe and the Soviet Union, he says democracy is the best hope society has to save the health of the planet.

The Hudson is his passion. He talks about it at length. The Hudson is the only remaining healthy estuary on the East Coast. It is an awesomely bountiful ecosystem, a place where bluefish from the ocean feed alongside largemouth bass from the fresh water tributaries. It is an ecosystem that attracts uncountable spawning fish, which discharge uncountable eggs and sperm, which form uncountable juvenile fish: striped bass, shad, blueback herring, alewives—anadromous fish, which live in salt water and breed in fresh. It is one of Bobby Kennedy's favorite words. "Anadromous," he exhorts his audiences. "Does anybody know what it is? Who can guess? OK, let's all say it. Anadromous. One, two, three: anadromous." Stripers caught in the Hudson and transported across the continent in the Nineteenth Century. And now that the Chesapeake Bay and the Delaware Bay and other great East Coast estuaries are too polluted to support much marine life, the Hudson may return to its historical role as "the Noah's Ark of the East Coast," he says.

He is a teacher, some would say a proselytizer. He asks an audience of middle school students what they think are the major problems facing the world. The answers come tentatively: Global warming. Destruction of the rain forests. Acid rain.

Nobody says nuclear war.

"The major preoccupation of my generation was that we were going to be taken over by the Russians," Bobby Kennedy says. He details the instructions he was given, at Our Lady of Victory, in Washington, D.C., about what to do when the bomb was dropped, and then segues into the national preoccupation with the military.

"As a result of that," he says, "we have created—my

102

generation and the people who are older than me—created a world where sixty percent of the money that our government spends is spent on military technology . . . every sixty cents of every tax dollar is spent on building military airplanes, jets and missiles and supporting our soldiers in Europe, Japan and the Philippines. Eighty percent of the scientists—eight out of every ten scientists—who are employed in the world are employed in building and developing weapons. The world altogether spends a trillion dollars a year building the military. That's two hundred dollars for every man, woman and child on the face of the Earth. We can no longer continue to expend those kind of resources on destructive weapons or destructive technologies, or on ways to destroy each other, if we're going to save the environment. We have to make a choice. We probably need to spend money defending ourselves but the major threat that I think your generation and my children will see is not going to be an invasion by the Russians, but it's going to be what's happening to the rain forest, it's going to be smog. You are probably not going to die from a Russian bullet. . . . You're going to understand that the most likely way for you to die before your time is because there's contaminants in the environment, because your drinking water is poisoned, because the air is poisoned, because of economic crisis that comes about from global warming.

"The major problem for all of us is going to be that the planet is going to be very different when you're my age from the planet that you grew up in—if we don't do something about it."

The urge to "do something about it" meant for his father trying to change things from the inside, through politics. His brother Joseph, sister Kathleen and cousin Patrick are attempting to change things through politics. But Bobby has no interest in politics. He is content to challenge the government from the outside. Yet, he says, the motive is the same one that drives his siblings and cousins, and sets them apart from most other rich kids.

David Kennedy
The Lost Son

Even in a close family, some are closer than others. In the Robert Kennedy family, according to intimates, it seemed that David, whose life ended tragically in his twenty-ninth year, had held a special place in his father's heart. Like his father, David was the fourth child and third son. Bobby seemed to consider this similarity a unique bond between them.

Intelligence, good looks, charm, competence, and competitiveness seem to be part of being born a Kennedy. But David did not exactly fit that mold. Although his intelligence and good looks were evident, the Kennedy fighting spirit seemed to have been modified by a special sensitivity and a very gentle nature.

David Anthony Kennedy was born on June 15, 1955, Ethel Skakel Kennedy's first child to be delivered by caesarean section. His middle name, also his patron saint, was his mother's choice: Saint Anthony of Padua, traditionally invoked for the recovery of lost articles.

In a household that stressed independence, excellence, and maximum effort in work and in play, David was always less assertive than his siblings. A close friend of the family recalled that Bobby was less demanding and more gentle with David, and that his voice seemed to soften when he spoke of this quieter child.

Like all his siblings, David's early schooling was at Our Lady of Victory School in Washington, D.C., not far from Hickory Hill, the family home in Virginia. In the Kennedy tradition, David played touch football and was coached in swimming and tennis. During the summers at Hyannis Port he also learned to sail. Although an agile athlete, he never seemed to share the Kennedys' extreme gusto for sports. Given the choice, David would often prefer to sit quietly and read. However, he seemed to enjoy the dinner-table discussions led by his father about subjects from Shakespeare to the history of the Civil War to events of current interest.

Bobby was a demanding parent; he was firm but always very affectionate with his children. A friend remembered a day when, in a moment of tension, Bob raised his voice to David. David burst into tears. His father immediately dropped to his knees and put his arms around the distraught little boy.

David was eight years old when his Uncle Jack was assassinated. In the months that followed, he had frequent nightmares in which he saw his father murdered. Being with his father became his highest priority. As one family friend put it, "Bobby's youngsters were always around him, but David was his constant shadow." Whenever RFK departed for a meeting or event at which his children could be included he would stand at the bottom of the stairs and call out to them, announcing where he was going and asking who wanted to go with him. One or another of David's brothers and sisters might decline the invitation on the grounds of homework or a scheduled activity, but, after JFK's death, David was always ready to go. It was as if he wanted to be sure that his father was safe.

When RFK was running for president, he and Ethel campaigned strenuously, which involved almost constant traveling. As the important California Democratic presidential primary approached, he became anxious to see his children and arranged for the six of them to be flown to Los Angeles. (A member of his staff still wonders if it was a premonition.) On Monday, June 3, 1968, the day before the vote, Bobby was exhausted. Nevertheless, he was determined that he and Ethel would take the children to the beach, where they spent the night at the Malibu home of film director John Frankenheimer.

The next morning, after roughhousing on the beach, RFK dashed into the ocean, David close on his heels. Within minutes, David was pulled beneath the water by the strong coastal undertow. His father dived down and pulled him out, but not before the child's forehead was badly bruised.

The family returned to the Ambassador Hotel and left the recuperating boy upstairs with author/historian Theodore H. White. A short time later, David sat with White in front of the television watching his father's victory speech. As the candidate left the room, pandemonium broke loose and viewers throughout the world —including David and White—heard the announcement that RFK had been fatally shot in the hotel kitchen on his way out to a victory party.

David, who turned thirteen eleven days after his father's death, retreated into silence and seemed inconsolable. His recurring nightmare had come true. As he had seen it over and over in his dreams, time and again on television he heard every aspect of his father's assassination described in excruciating detail. Ethel Kennedy, three months pregnant with her eleventh child, put all her considerable energies into comforting her children. The others gradually learned to cope with their loss. David never did.

Senator Edward M. Kennedy, Uncle Teddy, was devoted to all his nieces and nephews and determined to be a surrogate father to his brothers' children. He took them camping and invited them to events that might be appropriate or interesting for them; he made it a priority to attend birthday celebrations, graduations, and other significant occasions in their lives. But although he and David were friends, he couldn't exorcise the pain that seemed to engulf the adolescent boy.

Predictable Temptation

The traditions and expectations were a constant for all the Kennedy grandchildren, but with two of their fathers dead and one distanced by divorce, the kinds of discipline and strength that had kept their parents under strict control were not always in place for every member of the third generation. This was the late 1960s. It was almost predictable that some of the adolescent Kennedys would be tempted to experiment with drugs.

In the same way that their parents had been magnets for the mass media, the young Kennedys were subject to constant press scrutiny. Their every action and escapade were considered of interest to the public and thus fair game for the media. What might have been an insignificant episode in another family was all over the papers when a Kennedy was involved.

This created another form of pressure, and David seemed to find it intolerable. He became cynical and suspicious—always on guard against people he suspected might misuse the name of his father or his family.

David graduated from Milton Academy in 1973 and entered Harvard University. He was well-liked on campus and for a time managed to keep up with his classes. He also worked as an intern in his Uncle Ted's senatorial office in Boston—filing, doing case work, and, his uncle hoped, learning about the kinds of work his Uncle Jack and his father had found so compelling. As with his other nephews, Ted hoped to stimulate David's interest in public service. He would have David sit in on meetings with him and go to lunches and receptions, both as a learning experience for David and as an opportunity for them to spend time together. David seemed to thrive there and members of Ted Kennedy's staff experienced David as an "able and exceptionally kind and compassionate young man."

After what seemed a good start, David's grades fell and he received permission to withdraw from Harvard. RFK's friends, who had rallied—and remained— around Ethel, were eager to help the troubled young man. In February 1974, hoping to further David's interest in journalism, his father's friend John Seigenthaler, publisher of the *Nashville Tennessean* (now also editorial director of *USA Today*), offered him a job as a cub reporter. David worked for the *Tennessean* for over a year and did very well. According to Seigenthaler, "David could have been an outstanding journalist. He had an inquisitive mind and was not afraid of hard work. He learned quickly and had a remarkable and rare talent for writing a simple declarative sentence."

Although initially somewhat distant from his co-workers—Seigenthaler describes him as innately shy—David gradually warmed to his supervising editors and other staff members. Seigenthaler recalls that, "David had a remarkable diversity of interests." His bylined stories included coverage of subjects such as the environment, local government, country music, and miscellaneous human interest features on people and events.

For part of the time that he was in Memphis, David lived with the Seigenthalers. Seigenthaler and David would sometimes stay up late at night drinking as the publisher reminisced about his days with David's father. Seigenthaler is certain that David was not using drugs at that time.

Seigenthaler remembers a Sunday when his mother invited him, his wife, and David to lunch at her home. The elder Mrs. Seigenthaler mentioned that she wanted to show them a quotation in a book she knew she had, but couldn't seem to locate. A great believer in Saint Anthony—she called him "Tony"—she asked aloud for his help. David told her that Saint Anthony was his patron saint and that he was named after him. Later that afternoon, she found the missing volume on a nearby shelf. She was convinced that David had had a hand in its recovery. And David laughingly took credit for it.

He had an insatiable desire to learn about the lives of his father and uncle. One evening Seigenthaler asked David if he recalled visiting Nashville in 1968 when he and his brother Michael had accompanied their father for a campaign speech at Vanderbilt University. Although David had been twelve years old then, he had no recollection of ever being in Nashville. Seigenthaler took out a scrapbook and showed David several pictures of himself and his brother sitting between RFK and John Glenn on a platform before a crowd of 18,000 people. David pored over the pictures for a very long time. "It was," says Seigenthaler, "as if he were trying to get a fix on a valuable piece of history that he had forgotten."

Drugs and Disease

After leaving Nashville, David returned to Harvard, where he was a bright but erratic student. In 1976 his studies were interrupted by a bout with pneumonia. They ended a short time later when he developed pericarditis and endocarditis—severe infections of the membrane that surrounds the heart—which forced him to spend several months in Massachusetts General Hospital. It is probable that he was using drugs at that time, as this condition is a frequent cause of death in intravenous drug users.

David recovered from the near-fatal illness, but not from his addiction to drugs. Some of his cousins and his brother Bob were having their own struggles with drugs, yet they were able to win the battles and go on to lead productive and satisfying lives. That victory eluded David.

David intended to return to Harvard, but never did. He was seen about Manhattan with beautiful young women, frequenting discotheques and clubs. Still interested in writing, he completed a six-month internship at the *Atlantic Monthly.* He was capable, but couldn't seem to commit to any one project. His family spared no effort or expense to help him. In moments of cynicism, David questioned whether their concern was for his problems or for the publicity they generated. Yet, with their encouragement, he entered a variety of drug treatment programs in the United States and England. There were times when he seemed better, but they were only temporary.

Neither his family nor his friends could find the answer for David. No one was able to reach him. The years that followed were a series of failed efforts at treatment centers and halfway houses. David seemed to have decided that there were no answers anywhere. There were periods of promise, but his need for drugs was always more powerful.

A close associate of the family theorizes that if, like other young Kennedy males, "David had found the right girl, he would have been able to fulfill his marvelous potential." Another of David's mentors says, "David was not a bad boy. He was a good boy who used drugs because he hurt so much. If only he could have coped with his pain and survived, he would have made a great contribution."

Devoted to his grandmother, Rose Kennedy, David went to visit her in April 1984 in Palm Beach, Florida. As she had other house guests at the time, David opted to stay at a nearby hotel. It was there that he accidentally took the fatal combination of drugs that ended his life. On April 24, two months before his twenty-ninth birthday, away from his mother, his aunts and uncles, his ten brothers and sisters, and his eighteen cousins, David died alone in a room in a resort hotel. Saint Anthony, the finder of lost articles, had not been able to help David Anthony Kennedy find himself.

Courtney Kennedy

Although she always enjoyed the games and sports that went with being a Kennedy, it became clear at an early age that Courtney had inherited her mother Ethel Kennedy's love of children and home. It seems ironic that at 34, the quintessentially feminine Courtney, who always seemed more interested in family than a career, is without children and is separated from her husband.

Mary Courtney Kennedy was born on September 9, 1956, the fifth child of Ethel and Robert F. Kennedy, then Chief Counsel of the U.S. Senate Permanent Subcommittee on Investigations. Courtney had one older sister and three older brothers, and would be followed by six more siblings. The Robert Kennedy household revolved totally around the children. Although Hickory Hill, their home, had a recreation room, a heated swimming pool, stables, and acres to play on, the young Kennedys, their friends, toys, and books could usually be found in every room.

Bob and Ethel encouraged their children to excel in athletics, but were also intent on developing character and intellect. Religion, history, and the classics were frequently discussed at the dinner table. The children were included at the many parties and benefits that regularly took place at Hickory Hill, which helped them to develop poise at a young age. They dined frequently with U.S. officials, foreign ambassadors, and other dignitaries. But they also learned compassion as they were present at the numerous events their mother held for underprivileged children.

When her father was assassinated in 1968, the rather shy child RFK always referred to as "my beautiful Courtney" was eleven years old. Like her brothers and sisters, Courtney was desolate. But the older children had decided that the family had to present a brave front to the world, and Courtney tried to follow their example. Their father's charismatic presence had always been —and still is—a constant and profound influence on his children. He was able to roughhouse with them and still be a gentle but firm disciplinarian. Ethel believed in the standards he set, but could never duplicate the long, serious, and persuasive conversations that had been Bob's way of guiding and correcting his children.

Courtney started her schooling at Our Lady of Victory in Washington and went on to Potomac, a private school for girls not far from Hickory Hill. In the summer, she helped her mother take care of the inner-city youngsters who were often invited to the Kennedy home for a day of recreation, and also spent time at the Kennedy compound, visiting her grandparents and joining her cousins as they swam, sailed, played tennis, and trooped around Hyannis Port.

Following active and adventurous summers, such as working under the supervision of Mormons at a ranch in Utah, Courtney broke the Kennedy pattern of attending Eastern schools when she entered the University of California. Her education included studies in history and literature at Trinity College in Dublin, Ireland.

During college, she spent her summers working at the Robert F. Kennedy Memorial Foundation and also helped with her uncle Ted's 1980 presidential campaign and his 1982 campaign for reelection to the Senate, as well as working in the congressional campaigns of her brother and sister, Joe and Kathleen.

Courtney met television producer Jeff Ruhe while she was a production assistant for Children's Television Workshop. They were married in 1980 at Trinity Church in Georgetown. Courtney often accompanied Jeff on assignments such as coordinating ABC Television's coverage of the Winter and Summer Olympics. They were a popular couple, leading an active life, yet separated early in 1990 after ten years of marriage.

Although shy, Courtney has many friends, as well as close relationships with her siblings and her Kennedy cousins, especially Maria Shriver, Caroline Kennedy and Sydney Lawford. She enjoys painting and has lent her talents to Very Special Arts. She also has been a volunteer for the Head Start program. Considered one of the best fund-raisers in the family, Courtney is involved in many of the causes her family supports. She heads fund-raising for the Robert F. Kennedy Memorial Foundation, and is on the board of directors of the John F. Kennedy Library. Speaking of Courtney, a family friend said, "She is very beautiful and an unusually gentle, caring person."

Michael Kennedy

One to Watch

What could the congressman be thinking, leaning against his desk, looking at the young man sitting in front of him? The kid's wiry frame is draped leisurely across half the sofa, a blue pinstriped suit hanging loosely from his long-distance-runner's body. His tousled brown hair is short on the sides, a few strands flopping rebelliously across the part. When he smiles, there's a flash of those famous teeth, prominent in front and clustered oddly at the sides. All that's missing is the battered flight jacket, or the sea of hands reaching up to him. Outwardly, the congressman remains calm and composed, but inside? "My God, it's Bobby!"

In perfect prep-school English, the kid is inviting him to come on a trip to Africa. "We'll be going to Namibia, Angola, and the Congo, meeting with members of SWAPO. . . ." but suddenly he interrupts himself. ". . . Uhhhh . . . Uhhhh. . . ." More recent associations come to mind: Teddy on national TV, fumbling for a reason he . . . uh . . . uh . . . wants to be president.

Then, the kid starts talking again, "the only day you might miss votes is the Tuesday after Memorial Day, but, as you know, often there are no votes the day after recess." After the Interminable Pause is over, it is often something quite intelligent that spills out of the mouth of Michael Kennedy.

Who? No, not the sexiest man alive (that's John), nor the precocious one (that's Patrick, the 23-year-old Rhode Island state rep.), nor the one with a handicap (Edward Jr.). Without a doubt, you have never heard of this Kennedy. But the diplomatic 32-year-old middle child of the Robert Kennedy clan, Michael, is one to watch.

Living life as a Kennedy is not as easy as you might think. Sure, they're born with money, access, and off-the-charts name recognition. Today, there are dozens of them scattered about, poised to launch an all-out assault on the American political landscape. But, as Michael's older sister Kathleen discovered when she lost her bid for a Maryland congressional seat in 1986, success is far from guaranteed. Standing in the way is The Kennedy Myth.

The Myth, of course, is the divinity a nation has conferred on Jack and Bobby—envinced by the pictures of JFK that hang in many Catholic homes right next to Jesus Christ. It's one thing for a child to live up to the expectations of a successful father; it's something else entirely when his father is looked upon as a god. The next generation's dilemma—to which Teddy never found the answer—is, how can you ever prove yourself when you're a Kennedy?

The ideal strategy for all the children would be to lie low so they could grow up and make mistakes, just like everybody else, without having the world know about it. Publicity only tarnishes The Myth, giving some future opponent a campaign issue. But lying low was impossible for Robert F. Kennedy's notorious oldest sons, who had to grow up in full public view. Now, everyone knows that Bobby was a heroin addict, and David died of an overdose. The next son—and spitting image of his father—is Michael LeMoyne, who has managed to escape notice.

Michael's obscurity has more to do with circumstance than design. As the middle kid in a family of eleven, nobody paid much attention to him. The Boston media has run stories over the years about the Michael Kennedy who heads the school-bus union and the Michael Kennedy who invented a dog washer. But excepting a few celebrity reports on his marriage to Frank Gifford's daughter, Victoria, and birth announcements for each of three children, Bobby and Ethel's sixth child has remained almost invisible.

Even Boston insiders are surprised to learn that Michael is chairman of an international company that in 1988 had $850 million in sales, making it one of the highest-grossing firms in New England. He is now competing against the giant oil companies for drilling contracts throughout the world, especially in Africa, where his name has helped him develop close business relationships with many leaders of that oil-rich continent. If the African gamble pays off and his firm strikes crude oil, according to company president Wilber James, "This company might go KABOOM!—right through the roof."

One last surprise: the name of his company is Citizens Energy Corporation of Boston.

That's right, it's the same little boutique charity Joe started in 1979 to buy and sell oil and use the profits to lower the heating bills of the poor and elderly in Massachusetts. The nonprofit company that catapulted Joe to Congress in 1986 and, by all rights, should have allowed him to emerge from under the shadow of The Myth.

Joe had persuaded Venezuela's then-energy minister Humberto Calderon Berti to sell his new company two million barrels of crude oil at $31 a barrel, $6 below the OPEC price. It was a perfect public relations gesture for Venezuela, which shipped a vast majority of its petroleum products to the U.S. East Coast. Berti apparently was hoping the magnanimous gesture would show outraged Americans that the skyrocketing price of oil was not OPEC's fault, but the major multinationals. Citizens was guaranteed a healthy profit by the time it contracted to have the oil refined and sold.

Although never wildly profitable, Citizens Energy did manage to earn and give away about $26 million over the next ten years and land Joe favorable stories in *Mother Jones, Fortune,* and *People* magazines. By 1985, when Tip O'Neill retired from Uncle Jack's old congressional seat, Joe could accept the challenge with a clear conscience. He was a Kennedy who had done something. It seemed that he had finally discovered a way to beat The Myth. Not by running away, but by using it.

Meanwhile, his younger brother Michael quietly took over the company in 1984 and began remaking it in his more businesslike image. The first big change was for Citizens to plunge headlong into the risky world of foreign oil exploration.

The company is still struggling. But if Citizens strikes oil, it's not only some poor and elderly folks in the United States and abroad who will benefit. A gusher would also firmly establish this company as a Kennedy family proving ground.

If such a small charity, accounting for only about 2 percent of the total fuel assistance in Massachusetts, could launch Joe to a congressional seat, what might a big international conglomerate that strikes oil do for his younger brother? Not only does Michael have the Kennedy look. He also knows how to make The Myth work for him.

A Charmer at Work

So anyway, there stands Rep. Chris Shays, a Lowell Weickerish Republican, staring through wire-rimmed glasses at this eerie version of Bobby Kennedy, circa 1950, perched earnestly on a couch in his Washington, D.C., office. As it turns out, what the congressman had really been thinking about all this time was parades.

Michael wants Shays to come to Africa with him to show leaders of countries like Namibia and the Congo that giving the Kennedy oil company a drilling contract will also give them access to decision makers in Washington. Angola's communist president Jose Eduardo dos Santos, for example, hasn't gotten much respect from the last two administrations and would be more than happy for the chance to bend the ear of a congressman with his side of the story.

After dashing out to get his appointment book, Shays sits on the couch next to Michael and shakes his head sadly: That's Memorial Day weekend. Not a chance. Africa may be in turmoil, but he's got parades to go to. And every American politician knows hell hath no fury like a VFW post scorned.

Such are the obstacles Michael Kennedy is facing on this fine, cherry-blossomed spring day in the nation's capital. He had got out of bed early that morning while his kids, Michael LeMoyne Jr., Kyle Frances, and Rory, were still fast asleep, put on his blue pinstriped suit with a funky-colored tie, drove from his house in Cohasset to the dock at Hingham, where he grabbed the commuter boat to Logan Airport. He boarded a 7:50 a.m. USAir flight, carrying his battered brown briefcase and tan Burberry's trench coat, a lock of hair falling, classically Kennedyish, across his forehead. He travels alone, without assistants or entourage.

Clicking open his briefcase, he examined his typewritten itinerary for the day: a meeting with Charles Stalon, a member of the Federal Energy Regulatory Commission at 10 a.m., and then meetings with three congressmen before catching a 2 p.m. flight back to Boston to meet with A. E. Yoka, the Congo's minister of mines, energy and telecommunications.

When the plane touched down in Washington, Michael walked briskly through National Airport and ducked into a cab. It was only April, but already the air in Washington was warm and muggy.

"From Nigeria, driver?"

"Yes, from Benin," said the cabbie, glancing back through the rearview mirror, pleased that his worldly passenger had recognized his accent.

119

"I know a beautiful woman from Benin," said Michael. "Her name is Mary."

"Oh, is she your girlfriend?"

"I wish."

Michael is smooth in even casual conversation, coming in at precisely the right moment with a professional laugh, making the cabbie feel special. He opened his briefcase, took out a cellular phone, pulled up the antennae and began dialing.

"Are you calling Mary?" the cab driver laughed.

As it turns out, Michael was calling Mary, but not the same one. It was Mary Paris, his assistant back in Boston, to ask her to phone the energy commissioner and say that Michael is running a bit late. He was not really late, arriving at 10:03. But no matter, Michael race-walks through airports and the halls of Congress like a man on a mission. Which, of course, he is. Ostensibly, the mission is to beat the big multinational oil corporations in the energy business and use the profits to help the poor, both in America and developing nations. Michael says one reason his company is able to get drilling contracts in African nations is because it promises to reinvest 25 percent of its profits into development projects. So the company has set up a Citizens Farm in Nigeria and a fish-drying project in Angola.

This would seem in perfect keeping with the Kennedy legacy, and that's how Citizens Energy likes to be perceived—as a kind of modern, business-driven Peace Corps of the nineties. Not a welfare program, mind you, but a "business." And yet the legacy that the company relies on to open doors around the world is a curious melange of myth and reality, the untangling of which reveals how truly Kennedyesque this company is.

Joe Kennedy Sr.'s dynastic dreams had everything to do with power, ambition, and public relations and almost nothing to do with liberal causes like helping the poor. Or as Eleanor Roosevelt once said about Jack,

"Too much profile and not enough courage." Having a social conscience was not an important asset in the 1950s, when the patriarch was meticulously planning Jack's political career. And President Kennedy was hardly a leader on issues with which The Myth associates him, like civil rights. But, as his father used to say, "It's not what you are that counts, but what people *think* you are."

"Is that a wimp reason or what?" Michael Kennedy is talking into the phone again to Mary Paris. He's teasing her because Congressman Shays—Mary's ex-boss—had just declined the invitation to Africa.

After his disappointment with Shays, Michael stopped to make a few calls from the congressional office of his brother Joe, who was off at a press conference with Jesse Jackson. On the wall hangs a framed front page from the *Boston Herald* showing Joe, standing with his arms spread wide before a delirious election-night crowd, as if baptizing them. The headline blares, "KO for Joe K!" Nearby hangs a famous black and white 1968 campaign picture of his father reaching down to a sea of hands. And a big full-color photograph of Joe and Michael canoeing, a smiling Joe looking robust and daring in front, his excited little brother Michael in the back, steering.

Another phone rings, and a woman picks it up and says, "Oh, hello, Joe."

Michael looks up expectantly. "Is that Bro?"

Comparisons between Joe and Michael are inevitable. The only fair way to judge a Kennedy is by comparison to other Kennedys. They are a tiny civilization unto themselves, an elite tribe with their own rules, codes of behavior, and peculiar psychology. Competition among Kennedy siblings, especially the men, has always been fierce.

After hanging out in Joe's office for a while, Michael walks across Independence Avenue into the Capitol building to have lunch in the Members Dining Room with an old childhood friend named Juan, who is in the commercial real estate business. They both order Budweisers and club sandwiches and, for dessert, Michael consumes an enormous ice cream sundae, shoveling it down like a kid. They tell tall tales about their friends, like the crazy rugby player now in Australia who is "not human. His knuckles drag on the ground." They talk about windsurfing, about another friend buying some property in the Adirondacks, about how they've known each other since they were six years old. They laugh about the time in Hyannis when Juan dropped a water balloon from an upstairs window on Coretta Scott King, who was visiting the Kennedys soon after her husband was assassinated. "The newspapers asked my mother about it," says Michael, "and she said, 'Well, at least he had a good aim.' "

After finishing their lunch in the Members Dining Room, Michael and Juan walk toward the door. The place is full of tourists and lobbyists scanning the room for famous faces. One middle-aged woman in a black and white polka dot dress can't believe her eyes when she sees Michael coming. As he approaches her table, her eyes grow wider, as if she is seeing a ghost. She can't stop staring as he passes by, craning her neck so far back that by the time he's gone, she is looking straight up at the ceiling.

Growing up Reasonable

Michael was only ten years old when his father died, and as the sixth child was cushioned from many of the traumas that his older siblings had to endure. He was considered the most resilient child—"I guess I was the reasonable one," he says—and while his older brothers were getting into drugs and being kicked out of the house, he observed the chaotic scene with a kind of droll, preadolescent detachment. For a time, he would answer the phone by saying, "Confusion here."

The middle child in a big family is easily intimidated by his older brothers and sisters—they are bigger, smarter, and much cooler than he is. He badly wants to earn their respect, to be included in their sophisticated games, so he quietly drives himself to be better, smarter, faster. As he's in the middle, his movements go largely unnoticed. Then everyone is surprised when he becomes a success.

So it seems to be with Michael. Coming of age in the early eighties, he did not have nearly the same pressure to wear the liberal mantle that his older brothers did. Private-sector success was back in vogue. His generation was not expected to save the world, and that freed him to pursue his career in a measured, methodical way.

Michael was by no means a genius in school. But when he had some trouble with certain classes, he didn't get impatient and look for a way out. He calmly figured out what the teachers wanted and gave it to them, bringing his Bs and Cs up to As and Bs. He graduated from Harvard in 1980—in four consecutive years—and had the advantage of having a family business to go into after school, something the older kids never had. He worked at Citizens for a year, married in 1981, and followed his father's path by going from Harvard to law school at the University of Virginia.

By all accounts, Michael is a loyal younger brother, much as his father was. He quietly helped out with the campaigns of his Uncle Ted and sister Kathleen and played a major role in Joe's 1986 campaign.

Graduating from law school in 1984, Michael went to work for Hogan & Hartson, the Washington, D.C., law firm that represents Citizens. After a summer there, Joe asked him to come back to work at Citizens. "My dilemma was, 'Well, should I work for a firm in Washington and get more experience or work for Joe?' "

Michael says today, "A lot of that law firm's work was on Capitol Hill for various groups, so it was in a milieu that I was comfortable with and I thought would broaden me professionally."

At the time, Citizens was evolving from a small-time charity to a major-league business, so it posed a unique challenge for a kid just out of school wrestling with the Kennedy dilemma. In its early years, the company was run more like one of Uncle Ted's reelection efforts—a lot of volunteers and enthusiasm, cramped temporary office space, student-workers and a Kennedy cause to rally around. But when OPEC collapsed in 1983, oil prices tumbled, and the industry was thrown into chaos. Citizens Energy believed it had two choices: it could turn this shoestring operation into a real business, setting up for-profit subsidiaries, replace the students with some of the best technical experts in the field, and dive headfirst into the complex and risky business of trading oil futures. Or it could close up shop.

So Citizens set up a for-profit oil subsidiary, which launched into speculation on the risky oil futures market. Total sales went through the roof—from $167 million in 1983 to $726 million in 1985, but a large overhead made profit margins small, "significantly less than 1 percent," said Wilbur James. Only a trickle of free oil was left for the poor.

A little trickle is better than no trickle, of course, so Citizens' mission was still being fulfilled. But oil futures is a risky business, and the company wasn't doing a large enough volume to make a substantial profit. So it began to expand into other areas—selling pharmaceuticals by mail and marketing natural gas. Citizens Gas Supply Corp. is now one of the top ten independent natural gas marketers in the country and accounts for about half of the company's profits.

Today, the five taxable subsidiaries of Citizens Corporation include: Citizens Health Corporation, Citizens

Gas Supply Corporation, Citizens Resources Corporation, Citizens Power and Light Corporation, and Citizens Fuels Corporation. Additionally, the company has added a new (1990) for-profit venture called Citizens Housing Access which aims to get groups of low- and moderate-income residents to buy distressed buildings that have been foreclosed by banks. The program is run out of the same building in Boston that houses the other Citizens activities.

If there is an *eminence grise* at Citizens Energy, it is Wilber James, who has known Joe since they shared a Peace Corps tent in Kenya in their late teens. Now 43 and balding, with a droopy mustache, James quietly runs the for-profit businesses that drive the company. It has always been the job of the Kennedy boys to handle the high-level diplomatic and political work.

By the time Michael took over in 1985, diplomacy was becoming an increasingly important part of the business. Despite its claims to be a real business, the company has always relied heavily on the power of the Kennedy name. However, the magic failed to work in the tough business of oil futures trading, which is governed by a complex of forces beyond the influence of even the Kennedys. So the company decided to come back home to the safe haven of politics, where the name can still move mountains.

Michael and Wilber spent the better part of two years flying around the world trying to convince foreign heads of state to give them contracts to drill for crude oil. They teamed up with big companies with exploration capabilities, such as Unical, Conoco and the French company Total, and landed contracts in places like Aruba, the Congo and Angola.

Before Citizens could start drilling, it needed to win the right to drill. That's where Michael came in. "He has a tremendous ability to get along with world leaders," says James. "We'll go down to Angola, where he's on a first-name basis with President Santos. Or President Sassou-Nguesso of the Congo. Access is the key to our ability to survive these days. . . . Frankly, this company would not be here today if it weren't for Michael Kennedy."

The Kennedy name has been effective in opening the doors that often lead to contracts. Now if Michael can get a few congressmen to pass up their VFW parades, he'll have the added strength of a few American dignitaries in tow to demonstrate how important he is. And, he figures, more contracts will follow.

Michael has already successfully completed two goodwill trips with dignitaries in tow: one to Angola and Nigeria in November 1988, accompanied by four U.S. congressmen, the other to the Congo, Namibia and Angola in August 1989, with a 727 loaded with tons of medical supplies, thousands of sneakers, one congressman and a group of oil and telecommunications executives.

These impressive parties helped demonstrate young Kennedy's clout. At the time of the 1989 trip, Michael said to a *Boston Herald* reporter, "We are opening up a political dialogue and, on a humanitarian level, we are showing a gesture from America that we are truly interested in that part of the world."

Better Luck

"Three commitments and four or five 'yeah I want to comes,' " says Michael a few days later, after another trip to Washington. He is tallying up the score while sitting on his couch. Restless Joe never had a desk, and Michael hasn't bothered to get one for himself since he moved in. The office has a photograph and a small bust of his father and some finger paintings by his kids.

Michael had been on the phone a moment earlier trying to get tickets to see the rock group REM. A heavy medicine ball lies under a table, a football on a chair. The office is spare, he says, so he has room to horse around. He picks up the football as he talks, pump-faking with one hand and slapping it into his palm. In a family that values quarterbacks and receivers, Michael is a quarterback.

He's a fascinating mix of family qualities. In true Kennedy fashion, he can be excruciatingly long-winded and unfocused when discussing legal and abstract issues. Ask him, for example, how his meeting with the federal energy commissioner went, and he says:

> Actually, he was fairly philosophical about the ability of regulators to operate in a changing . . . uh . . . uhhhhhhhh . . . economic environment. We really can't do much . . . uh . . . you know, it's only when you're dealing with a straight monopoly that we can see the whole piece of the puzzle here, that, uh, we're able to, uh, latch onto something. . . .

But ask him about the politics of the Energy Commission, and he sounds like Bobby, the inside player in Jack's administration, describing who's on their side, who's opposed, and where the alliances fall. Talk about cutting deals with energy ministers of exotic lands and his eyes light up as he tells of the adrenaline high that comes with taking on the big oil companies and winning.

One wonders, however, if Michael is capable of the kind of transformation his father went through. Late in life, Bobby began reading the French existentialist writer Albert Camus, visiting impoverished homes in the Mississippi Delta, and saying things like, "If I hadn't been born rich, I'd probably be a revolutionary."

Michael displays the more typical Kennedy aversion to introspection when asked about the moral choices he faced in deciding what to do with his life. He was asked the same question when he spoke at the University of

Virginia Law School, at a forum on his father. "Those students have to make this tremendous choice," he recalled. " 'Should I go to work for a public defender for $25,000 or should I work for $75,000 at a big New York firm?' That is a tremendous dilemma. 'Or should I go to work for some environmental concern?' And I didn't have a very good answer for them." Michael, who proceeded to pass the question off on another panelist, clearly hadn't given the matter much thought.

It's not the kind of question that would occur to someone who has never been faced with such a choice. Kennedys can do socially redeeming work *and* be rich— all at the same time. Which is what makes Citizens the perfect Kennedy enterprise, a place where James can use expressions like "2 plus 2 equals 7," Joe can ramble on about "win-win situations," and no one finds it odd. It was, no doubt, a "win-win" situation when Citizens moved to its current offices on Atlantic Avenue on Boston's waterfront—so Joe cruised to work in his boat, from his eleven-room colonial-style farmhouse in Marshfield.

"If you must go out and make a living, without any real meaning to it, it's not nearly as exciting as if you have a cause," said James, talking about the 80 people who work in their chic exposed-brick wall offices. "So we combine the cause with trying to make sure people here make a good living. Because we don't want them to suffer individually."

Michael's smooth manner and quick climb up the ladder are more reminiscent of his Uncle Jack. Unlike his older brother, Michael does not complain about what a ball of molasses the government is. He says he loves Washington and would like to work there some day. His ambition seems surprising for such an obscure Kennedy, but it seems that nobody had ever asked him about it before.

"Getting down to Washington has a lot of appeal to me," he says, slapping the football. "But I'm not on this fast track that has to happen tomorrow. And the reality is that Massachusetts had a few corks in the bottle up top. Things are moving pretty quickly, so I would not rule anything out, even in the short term. Some folks say I should be out there a little more often, that maybe I should be doing more to get my name in."

Nor is Michael averse to following his brother's lead in using the famous name on billboards to drum up support for Citizens Energy—something that brought flak to Joe because the signs appeared just before he announced his candidacy for Congress. For example, Michael may need some publicity for the company's new program to pick up trash from businesses, recycle it, and promote recycling in general. "I certainly would utilize whatever reputation I gained to ask people to participate in the program," he says. "So if that gains me some grief from somebody saying, 'Oh, he's just doing what his brother did,' who gives a . . . ?"

The use of the Kennedy name can be problematic. Employees of Citizens Energy recognize the value of the Kennedy name, yet they also expect credit and recognition for their contribution.

"I'm not a prop," complained Wilber James about a photographer who wanted to shoot him with Michael Kennedy, but not by himself. James has company among others slaving away in the trenches who have to live with the reality that the credit goes to the Kennedys. His complaint sounds like those who work in the state fuel-assistance program who say that Citizens contributes only a small fraction of the oil the state gives away to the poor. Such people would have been regarded as losers by Joe Kennedy Sr.—unless they could get a good PR agent. *(It's not what you are that counts.)*

Michael's grandfather was perhaps the nations' first spin doctor, a political visionary who seems to have intuited the American people's obsession with image before television and advertising proved it. If he were alive today, he would no doubt understand the political necessity of a social conscience—and that a pure lunge for power would be most unseemly for a Kennedy. He would have loved the photo opportunity that had Joe posed in front of the tankers bringing their cargo of free heating oil for the poor.

And if he could see Michael hustling through the airport in Washington, getting to know congressmen and bureaucrats, flying around the planet to cut deals with world leaders, developing an excellent track record by running a successful business that does some good in the world, and keeping on top of all the hot issues of the next decade like water conservation and trash, he would probably grin widely. Michael is one grandson who understands the path a Kennedy takes to power.

Grandfather himself couldn't have planned it any better.

Kerry Kennedy Cuomo
It's the Cause that Counts

A Kennedy wedding is always news. So there was much press speculation about the political implications of the union of Mary Kerry Kennedy and Andrew Mark Cuomo, the son of New York Governor Mario Cuomo on June 9, 1990. Was the couple's common bond that they had come from families so much in the public eye? In one of her rare interviews, Kerry offered a more conventional explanation. She said, "He's the man I love."

Mary Kerry Kennedy, the seventh child of Ethel and Robert Francis Kennedy, was born on September 8, 1959. Ethel and her children had been summering at Hyannis Port, and Robert, who was in Washington working to finish his first book, *The Enemy Within*, flew up to greet his third daughter.

According to her godmother, "From early infancy, Kerry was delightful, full of energy, and bubbling with enthusiasm. With dark eyes and blond hair, she had a *joie de vivre* that made her beautiful." She adds, "Kerry always seemed more independent than her older sisters, and even as a small child had very definite ideas about what she wanted to do and how she would do it." Her father was enchanted by his little individualist.

Growing up at Hickory Hill, in Virginia, Kerry learned quickly to compete in the touch football, tennis and family swimming matches that were a part of life there. She later noted that the athletic competition was her parents' way of teaching their children to do things together, to cooperate, and to excel. Although the rivalry among the siblings and cousins could be fierce, it was always understood that when outsiders were present, it was invariably "us against them."

With its expanse of grounds, its tennis courts, stables and heated swimming pool, Hickory Hill was always a gathering place for the young Kennedys and their friends. Remembering the days when the eleven children were usually around, a friend said, "I'll never forget the dogs—all the kids loved them and there were always what seemed like dozens of dogs all over the place, including in the house." A contemporary of one of the younger Kennedys remembers, "It was wonderful to go to Hickory Hill. All the kids were great. Even the older ones showed an interest in you just because you were their sibling's friend." She added, "It upsets me when I read unkind gossip about the Kennedy kids. They weren't perfect—they were human. But they're really nice people."

Robert and Ethel Kennedy designated each of their older children to be responsible for one of the younger ones. Kerry was Kathleen's special charge. Kerry was in the cousins group that included her sister Courtney and Caroline Kennedy, Kara Kennedy, Maria Shriver, and Sydney and Victoria Lawford.

At the Roman Catholic nuptial mass for Kerry and Andrew at St. Matthew's Cathedral in Washington, their attendants—two maids of honor, best man, bridesmaids, flower girls, ring bearer, ushers, and groomsmen—totaled forty-one, most of them relatives of the bride or groom. Kerry was a radiantly beautiful bride. The reception that followed was, of course, at Hickory Hill.

At the reception, a friend was asked if Kerry had dated a lot when she was growing up. The response was, "It's hard to say. There were always so many cousins and friends around that you couldn't tell if anybody was anybody else's date. They went out in bunches."

While religion is very important to all the Kennedys, some are more observant than others. Kerry has always been among the more deeply religious and considers her faith a source of strength and guidance.

Bob and Ethel set high standards for their children. They expected excellence in school, sports, and demeanor. The young Kennedys may have been boisterous among themselves, but when company came they knew that they had to be dressed up and on their best behavior. They were encouraged to join in discussions on numerous subjects, ask questions about anything at all, and to express their views—controversial or not. Both parents were dedicated to public service, and they helped their children understand the value of compassion. Kerry has conjectured that her present focus on human rights may have taken root when she was seven or eight years old and watched civil rights demonstrations and anti-war protests on television and heard her father discussing them at the dinner table.

In 1968, three months before her ninth birthday, Kerry's father was shot. In the decades that followed, numerous memorials honored Robert Kennedy, but his family's immediate task was to learn to live without him. Kerry and her sisters and brothers tried to comfort their mother as she waited for Rory, the baby girl born six months after her father's death. In time, laughter was heard again at Hickory Hill.

Kerry had begun school at Our Lady of Victory in Washington, D.C., where many of her brothers and sisters had also started, and then followed her sister Courtney to Potomac, a private school in suburban Virginia. Graduating in 1977 from Putney School in Vermont, she entered Brown University. Before finishing there, she took time off to work in the 1980 presidential campaign of her uncle Ted. Starting as a fund-raiser in his New York office, she later traveled around the country as a surrogate speaker. She proved an able and versatile spokesperson, covering topics that ranged from her uncle's policy on education to his concern about programs for the elderly.

Kerry graduated from Brown in 1982 and went to

work for a news photography agency in New York. She also became an active volunteer for Amnesty International, where she compiled information on the problems of refugees from war-torn El Salvador. Late in 1983, she traveled there to see firsthand the condition of human rights in that part of the world. She was deeply impressed by the young lawyers she met who had committed themselves to helping people who couldn't pay for the legal services they desperately needed. Then and there, Kerry decided that law school would be the best preparation for what she wanted to accomplish in the future.

Kerry enrolled at Boston College Law School, her cousin Chris Lawford's alma mater, and later interrupted her studies to work on her brother Joe's congressional campaign. While at his headquarters, she exchanged information and advice with her sister Kathleen Kennedy Townsend, who was running for Congress in Maryland. Both showed promise and though Kathleen lost, Joe prevailed.

Kerry's travels have included a trip to India, where she observed efforts to help local artisans adapt their skills and talents to larger projects aimed at helping them rise above subsistence living. Whenever she travels, Kerry makes it a point to learn about local conditions, the status of human rights, and the ways in which U.S. policy affects the country she is visiting.

Returning to law school, she graduated and passed the Massachusetts bar. Having become deeply involved with the Robert F. Kennedy Memorial, she decided to make it her primary focus. Aside from the family connection, it fit perfectly with her determination to serve as an advocate for human rights. Kathleen chairs the board of the Memorial, which is dedicated to carrying on the work to which their father pledged himself. Its programs include the Robert F. Kennedy Journalism Award, established in 1968 to recognize outstanding

print and broadcast media coverage of the problems of
the disadvantaged in America; and the Book Award,
established in 1980, to reward authors whose works
have reflected Robert F. Kennedy's concern for the
poor and powerless and his dedication to honest and
even-handed justice.

Kerry started as the Memorial's legal counsel and focused on the problems of international human rights. In
1988, she founded and became executive director of the
Robert F. Kennedy Center for Human Rights, operated
under the auspices of the Memorial that monitors human rights abuses around the world. Once a year, on or
about November 20th, Robert Kennedy's birthday, the
Center's Human Rights Award is presented to individuals who have made significant contributions to the struggle for human rights. The Center's International
Advisory Committee of forty distinguished human rights
advocates includes Archbishop Desmond Tutu of South
Africa; Carlos Fuentes, Mexican author, lawyer and diplomat; and Polish author and Nobel Prize Winner Czes-
law Milosz. Five American panelists make the final
selection; among them are Rose Styron, Chair of the
Advisory Council of Amnesty International USA and
Patt Derian, Assistant Secretary of State for Human
Rights in the Carter administration.

Kerry's bylined accounts of the Center's award to a
Korean husband and wife who had brought worldwide
attention to the torture of political prisoners in South
Korea, appeared in leading newspapers in Boston, Chicago, and elsewhere. Both the award to the Korean couple and a similar one to an unusually effective civil
rights lawyer in Kenya had to be presented in the recipients' countries, as their governments would not permit
them to leave. An informed observer notes that the
award has benefits that extend far beyond its presentation, that it illuminates and furthers the efforts of the

recipients. It also may help to insure their safety in sometimes dangerous political climates.

Newspaper publisher John Seigenthaler, a close friend of Bob Kennedy, continues to be devoted to Ethel and her children. He was chairman of the Robert F. Kennedy Book Award and is familiar with Kerry's work at the Center for Human Rights. He says, "Kathleen was at the Memorial first and she has done a marvelous job. But I feel Kerry has brought to it a very special vitality. Both of those young women, as well as their brother Joe and some of the others, make it clear that Bob's children—each in a different way—embody the elements of their father's character and personality, and reflect an awareness that they are heirs to a very great legacy."

Seigenthaler added, "They suffered a tragic loss when they were very young, and they have had their problems. But they have come out beautifully. Some of them have already begun to make valuable contributions. I have real confidence that the others will too."

A 1963 photograph taken in the Oval Office of President John F. Kennedy shows two cherubic little girls, Caroline Kennedy and Kerry Kennedy, peeking out from under the president's desk. The most recent photograph that appeared in the press shows the two young women amid their aunts, uncles and cousins—many with their spouses and children, at the celebration of the one hundredth birthday of their grandmother, Rose Fitzgerald Kennedy. Caroline is now a lawyer and the mother of two; Kerry, a dedicated worker for human rights.

RFK would have been very pleased.

Christopher Kennedy

Parents with countless kids must endure years of seemingly endless birthday parties. Thus, the birth date of Christopher Kennedy may have come as a relief. He was born in 1963, on the Fourth of July, twelve years to the day after his sister, Kathleen.

Just as Kathleen came to be the senior figure among the first seven siblings, Chris emerged as the leader of the youngest four. Though not quite five years old when he lost his father, young Chris instinctively took on a protective role toward his pregnant and heartsick mother. Friends were touched to see the little boy striving to comfort and take care of his usually inexhaustible mother. His seemingly paternal attitude also extended to his younger brothers, Max and Douglas, and younger sister Rory, born six months after his father's death. When guests arrived, it was often Chris who would welcome them and make sure their needs were attended to. He also tried to help his mother keep a semblance of order in the home. Although there was a household staff, no amount of help seemed adequate to keep up with the turmoil that could be created by eleven energetic children. Showing a maturity beyond his years, it was Chris who stepped in and delegated clean-up tasks to his brothers and sisters, even the older ones.

During his high school years, Chris devoted much of his free time to a center for runaway children. He was a sympathetic telephone counselor and would often take one of the troubled youths home. He was described as one of the most dedicated and effective young people who ever worked there.

Chris could play as hard as he worked, and was an enthusiastic competitor in family sports at Cape Cod. It was at Hyannis Port that Chris started his career as an entrepreneur. He operated a flourishing sailboat rental business which soon made it clear that he had a head for commerce.

Chris majored in political science at Boston University. After graduating in 1986, he moved to Chicago, where he joined the Merchandise Mart, a major furniture and trade center owned by the Kennedys. After three years of full-time work as director of the building products department, he began an MBA program at Northwestern University, while continuing to work part time at the Merchandise Mart.

In August 1987, he married Sheila Berner, a graduate of Boston College who went on to practice law in Winnetka, Illinois. Their first child arrived three years later.

True to his family's tradition for philanthropic volunteering, Chris raises funds for the Greater Chicago Food Depository, which works with wholesalers to provide food for almost 500 soup kitchens. Additionally, he is a volunteer fundraiser for El Valor, an organization that serves members of Chicago's Hispanic community who suffer from mental retardation.

Max Kennedy

Matthew Maxwell Taylor Kennedy was born on January 11, 1965, the ninth child and fifth son of Robert F. and Ethel Skakel Kennedy. His mother chose his first name. His father added the names of his good friend Gen. Maxwell Taylor, a much-decorated soldier and diplomat. Robert Jr.—almost eleven years older—considered Max his special charge, but Christopher, eighteen months Max's senior, was his constant companion. Max and Chris went through childhood virtually inseparable.

As Max grew up, his mother entertained frequently, especially on behalf of family charities. Max learned to feel at ease with adults. But he also reached out to the disadvantaged children who were invited to Hickory Hill each summer. He joined in most of the sports, but not riding, as he was allergic to horses. Max attended Moses Brown in Providence, Rhode Island, and graduated in 1983. He then went to Harvard University, becoming the fifth of RFK's children to enroll there. His major was American History and he received his degree in 1988. Having become interested in journalism, he spent a year in California working for the *Santa Monica News*. Earlier, he had interned in the press office of his uncle Ted. A staff member who knew him there describes Max as "a hard worker . . . intellectually curious and analytical . . . warm and thoughtful . . . charming, with a delightful sense of humor."

Unlike his cousin Maria Shriver, Max did not choose journalism as his career. However, through journalism he discovered environmental law, and followed his father to the law school of the University of Virginia. Today, he is involved with family causes and is active with the Robert F. Kennedy Memorial. Summers often find

Max at Hickory Hill with volunteer counselors, greeting busloads of children as they arrive five days a week to enjoy a day in the country.

"Max," a family friend says admiringly, "is a wonderful young man. He has always had a lovely disposition. Everyone likes him."

Douglas Kennedy

Douglas Harriman Kennedy, born on March 24, 1967, the tenth child of Robert and Ethel Kennedy, was named for two very distinguished statesmen, C. Douglas Dillon, his uncle's Secretary of the Treasury, and W. Averell Harriman, who served many presidents. "Although he was the baby of the family, even when he was a little boy, Dougie seemed especially concerned about others," a longtime friend remarked.

The older children in the RFK family remembered playing with their father and going with him to his office, and visiting the White House when their Uncle Jack was president. But Douglas wasn't even born then, and was just over a year old when his own father was assassinated. He has no memory of Camelot, so he has had to get his information second hand. His uncle Ted, who was determined to give all his brothers' children an understanding and appreciation of how John and Robert Kennedy had lived and what they had accomplished, patiently answered Dougie's countless questions.

All the young Kennedys went to mass regularly, but Douglas seemed to pray with a special fervor. As he grew up, he was kind and sensitive and genuinely eager to help anyone who had a problem. A strong believer in the effectiveness of prayer, he always lent his support and said special prayers on behalf of those he knew were ill or in need of help.

One of his contemporaries noted, "Dougie was always a really neat kid. He never knew that being a Kennedy gave him any special status. He was a real friend."

Douglas attended Potomac, a private girls school not far from his family's home in Virginia that began accepting boys in the mid-1970s, and went on to high

141

school at Georgetown Prep. He entered Boston College and then transferred to Brown, where he majored in English and philosophy and graduated in 1990.

Confirmed activists, Douglas and his sister Rory joined the protesters who picketed against apartheid in front of the Embassy of South Africa in the late 1980s. A member of the Community for Creative Nonviolence, Douglas worked at Mitch Snyder's shelter for the homeless in Washington's inner city. He was an anonymous member of the huge crowd that attended Snyder's funeral in the summer of 1990.

At this date, Douglas is undecided about his career. He has not indicated that he plans to follow members of his family to law school or to pursue elective office. He has an interest in writing, but has not declared it his career. However, he has made it clear that, like his father and other members of his family, he intends to do what he can to make a contribution to society.

Rory Kennedy

At the outset of labor, Ethel Kennedy knew that this child, her eleventh, would be her last. During delivery, Ted Kennedy stood in for his late brother Bobby, an act of affection that also imparted starkly that this newborn would never know her father.

Rory Kennedy was born seventeen years after Kathleen, the eldest child of Ethel and Bobby, and several months after her father was assassinated. At birth, she added one more to the number of her generation of Kennedys who were to grow up in a one-parent household. Yet Rory finds no need to dwell on what might have been. Instead, gratitude flows easily out of her for what family life was able to be.

"I didn't ever *consider* the idea that family could be a bad place or that a person could have bad experiences," Rory says. "The support and love of my family has just been a natural thing for me. It was always there."

Though her father's embrace was denied her, Rory finds him alive in the memory of strangers. "Of course, I'm sad I didn't know my father, but it's nice to hear so many stories about how he had meaning for people in their lives. My reaction to my father's death was never anger: more sadness, wondering, and at times, frustration."

Rory is twenty-two years old and completing her senior year as a liberal arts major at Brown University, in Providence, Rhode Island. Her cousin John was the first of her generation to attend this Ivy League School, followed by Rory's brother Douglas, a year ahead of her.

Rory has imbibed the family's biblically-based ethic—inherited through her mother from her grandmother Rose—that for life to have balance, it must be lived for a purpose beyond oneself. The Robert F. Kennedy Memorial Center for Human Rights provides Rory with a public service outlet. She has journeyed with her sister Kerry, the Center's executive director, to support El Salvadorans in opposition to Reagan administration policies. And in May of 1988, she likewise traveled to South Korea with her sister to present the 1987 Human Rights Award of the Robert F. Kennedy Memorial Center to Kim Keun-tae, a political activist serving a five-year sentence on charges of trying to topple the government of former president Chun Doo Hwan.

Not that Rory seeks to be relentlessly self-sacrificing: "I think I have a responsibility to myself to do whatever makes me happy. I don't, for example, feel that I have to do something in the political realm if I don't want to." Yet like most Kennedys, Rory works hard when she's hard at work and plays hard when she's hard at play. She enjoys skiing, and packs several years into every summer, such as recently when she worked as an apprentice to a sports photographer in Colorado, then headed west to break bread with Cesar Chavez as he finished a 36-day fast.

Among her cousins, Rory is a year younger than Patrick Kennedy and Amanda Smith, and only older than one cousin, Kym Smith. Did she ever feel lost as the youngest among so many siblings and cousins? With her hand, Rory smooths her long blond hair to the side and explains, "It was great; always exciting. By having so many brothers, I think I learned about life quicker. They would tell me, 'Don't do this because such-and-such a thing will happen.' I wouldn't always listen to them, but eventually I would usually find out they were correct."

After her husband was shot, Ethel rose to the occasion. Rory says, perky with admiration, "My mother is amazing. She is always there for me and for anybody.

She's so strong and comfortable with every aspect of herself and her surroundings. Hers is an expression of happiness and laughter and forward-going in all circumstances. She is always able to see the best in a person and in a situation."

One thing Rory did not fully enjoy as a child was her mother's mandatory Sunday night poetry readings. But now, finding enjoyment from the poetry of Yeats, T.S. Eliot, and Robert Frost (though Emily Dickinson is "a bit weird"), Rory is glad for the early exposure.

Ethel Kennedy also succeeded in imparting a reverence for the bible to this youngest of eleven kids. "I put religion right after family as a source of power and holding on," says Rory. "My mother is a very committed Catholic, yet is also open to any bible interpretation you might have. If I came home and said I was really interested in Hinduism, she would have an open mind."

Rory's family experience—and heritage—has brought a sense of security and self-confidence to this young woman. Should she in accordance with Kennedy tradition choose to mold her life into one with a public commitment, she will find that her family has provided her with the inner resources.

CHAPTER FIVE

THE CHILDREN OF
JEAN KENNEDY
AND
STEPHEN SMITH

*Jean Smith (1928–) married finan-
cier Stephen Smith, who was for
many years a close family advisor.
Smith died in 1990. Jean initiated a
summer day camp program for people with mental retardation at the
Smith's upstate New York retreat.*

Stephen Jr. (1957–)
William (1960–)
Amanda (1967–)
Kym (1972–)

Stephen Smith Jr.

Everyone who knows him agrees that Stephen Smith Jr. has inherited both his father's keen political acumen and his mother's concern for public service. Born on June 28, 1957, the first child of Jean and Stephen Smith, his childhood was much like that of his Kennedy cousins. He went to private schools in New York and during holidays and vacations often went to his parents' retreat in the Hudson Valley of New York, where the Smiths operated a summer camp for people with mental retardation. Steve's father was always considered the forceful member of the family; his mother is looked upon by her children and their cousins as unfailingly gentle and understanding.

Steve is the Smith who has shown the most interest in politics and world affairs. He is also a strong athlete: in addition to tennis, hockey and skiing, he has run in marathons and boxed. At the Kennedy family compound at Hyannis Port, Steve was one of the first to be chosen when the cousins divided into teams for sports.

Steve's activities have varied: he has been active in his mother's Very Special Arts Program for mentally and physically disabled children, worked in the campaigns of his Uncle Ted, and served as a legislative aid to Sen. Paul Simon (D-Ill). His primary focus has been somewhat different from the rest of his family: he has taken a particular interest in the people and politics of developing countries.

He graduated from Collegiate, a private school in New York City, and enrolled at Harvard University. Eager to learn more about his Uncle Bobby's life, Steve and a friend went to South Africa one summer and duplicated the itinerary RFK had followed when he visited that country in 1966. After graduating from Harvard in 1979, Steve worked in Thailand in a resettlement camp that housed refugees from Vietnam and Cambodia. With his exceptional ear for language, Steve learned Thai in the six months he was there. Although he remained outwardly unemotional, he was profoundly moved by the way the refugees were able to overcome the tragedies they had seen and endured.

On returning to the United States, Steve decided that a law degree would be valuable preparation for the areas of public service that concerned him. He enrolled at Columbia Law School and, like nine of his cousins, is now a lawyer. In 1982, Steve and his brother William took a crash course in Spanish and went to Costa Rica. They were deeply moved to learn that even in Costa Rica the Kennedy name was still remembered and revered. Working with a social service and political agency there reinforced Steve's commitment to public service. To this day, when Steve and William want to have a private conversation, they switch to Spanish.

Steve is now an instructor in international relations at Harvard. Still a bachelor, he lives in Cambridge. Although he has shown no inclination to run for office, an informed Kennedy observer predicts that "Steve will always be an integral part of his family's political activities."

William Smith

William Smith, the second son of Stephen and Jean Smith, was born on September 4, 1960. His parents identified closely with the Kennedy family ethic and tradition and passed that on to their children. His father, Stephen Sr., was an integral member of the Kennedy brain trust and one of the family's key strategists.

The Smiths often joined their relatives at the Kennedy family compound in Hyannis Port. Three years older than William, Stephen Jr. was the greater competitor; Willy enjoyed sports, but not to the same extent. The young Smiths also spent time at Pawling, New York, where their parents had a vacation home that they frequently converted to a summer camp for people with mental retardation. At Hyannis Port the boys learned to be team players; at Pawling they learned compassion.

William was always a good student. He attended Salisbury School in Connecticut and enrolled in Duke University, graduating in 1983. While at Duke he spent a term in London, where he prepared a report on race relations in England, focusing on the events that led to the infamous race riots in Brixton. He was a frequent observer at meetings and conventions of the newly formed Social Democratic Party. Later on, he traveled by train through much of Europe and Russia. He also went to China, where he learned enough of the language to carry on simple conversations.

His other travels include a memorable 1982 visit to Costa Rica with his brother, Steve. Both boys were deeply interested in family history and both spoke Spanish. They were overwhelmed to hear of the warmth and admiration with which many Costa Ricans regarded their uncles. When Corazon Aquino supplanted the discredited dictator Ferdinand Marcos in the Philippines, William's Uncle Ted sent him to Manila with his cousin Ted Jr. to gather first-hand information on the political situation and the status of democracy in that country.

William has been very active in the political and public service endeavors of his family. He has worked in several of Ted's campaigns and has volunteered with his Aunt Eunice's Special Olympics. In addition, he has been extremely active in both the New York and Washington offices of his mother's Very Special Arts program.

In view of his strong interest in art and the Kennedy propensity for law and politics, it is noteworthy that William Smith chose to become a physician. To date, the only Kennedy grandchild to have gone into medicine, William is now in his fourth year of medical school at Georgetown University in Washington, D.C., and plans to practice in community medicine as an internist. As avocations, William has been drawn to science and the arts. His paintings and drawings are prized possessions of many Kennedy relatives.

William's father died during the summer of 1990. Speaking at the funeral at St. Thomas More's Church in New York, William expressed his own and the Kennedy family's love and admiration for this talented man.

William is devoted to his family, and very warm to his friends. He tends to be reserved and is so protective of his privacy that newspaper pictures of William with his cousin John have been captioned, "John F. Kennedy Jr. and friend."

Amanda Smith

Stephen and Jean Smith felt themselves very blessed. They had a loving family, mutual interests, shared ethical values, financial security, a successful vocation, and gratifying avocations, not to mention their two fine sons. And then, on April 30, 1967, Amanda Mary Smith was born. As her brothers Stephen and William were, respectively, ten and seven years older than she, for five years, until the arrival of her sister, Kym, Amanda was the baby of the family. However, she is the same age as Douglas and Patrick Kennedy, and during the summers when many of the twenty-nine Kennedy grandchildren gathered at Hyannis Port, she and these cousins became special friends. She quickly excelled at touch football and the other sports that are on the family's agenda, and has become an expert horsewoman.

Amanda was always a good student. While attending Spence, a private New York City school for girls, she was invariably on the honor roll. She has a flair for languages and became fluent in French when she participated in an exchange program that took her to Paris during high school.

Following in the footsteps of seven of her Kennedy cousins, Amanda attended Harvard, where she received a Bachelor of Arts degree. During her undergraduate years, she spent a term in England at Oxford University, the only Kennedy cousin to have matriculated there. She is now back at Harvard working toward a Ph.D. in special education. The needs of special children have been the focus of many members of her family, but Amanda is the first to pursue an advanced degree in that field.

Like her brother William, Amanda is considered a

talented artist. Their paintings and drawings are favorite gifts within the family. One of the less public of the Kennedy cousins, Amanda has been described as brilliant but somewhat shy. She is dedicated both to her studies and to her work with children, and also to her family and friends.

Kym Smith

At the end of the 1960s, it appeared that the roster of Kennedy grandchildren was complete. Twenty-eight of the twenty-nine members of the third generation were born between 1951 and 1968, but four years later, the last of the third generation of Kennedys arrived. Born on November 29, 1972, Kym Maria Smith is the daughter of Jean Kennedy and Stephen Smith. As they had with their sons, Steve Jr. and Willy, the Smiths nurtured in both girls an ardent interest in learning, a desire for excellence, and a strong conviction that service to others should be an integral part of their lives.

Kym has always been as outgoing and gregarious as her sister, Amanda, is reserved and quiet. At an early age, Kym was eager to join her big brothers and older cousins in the rigorous pastimes that were an integral part of life at Hyannis Port, where the Kennedys, Shrivers, Smiths and Lawfords gathered each summer. She is an excellent athlete, proficient in tennis, swimming and riding.

Popular with her cousins and her many friends, Kym is considered the chatterbox of the family. The only Kennedy grandchild who still lives at home, she attends Marymount, a private high school for girls in New York City. Kym is a good student, participates in school activities, and also helps with Very Special Arts, the program her mother founded to provide an enjoyable and therapeutic means of expression for mentally and physically disabled individuals.

Innately curious about almost everything, Kym never stops asking questions. Unlike the older members of the third generation of Kennedys who remember visits to the White House when their Uncle Jack was president,

Kym and her younger cousins know political Washington only through their uncle Teddy, who often stays at the Smith home when he is in New York and is one of Kym's favorite sources of information.

Although it is too early for Kym to know what she will do in later life, it is reasonable to predict that this Kennedy grandchild will become an accomplished and contributing member of society. Pictures of the celebration of the 100th birthday of Rose Fitzgerald Kennedy show a smiling Kym in the front row among her cousins.

CHAPTER SIX

THE CHILDREN OF
JOAN BENNETT
AND
EDWARD KENNEDY

Edward M. Kennedy (1932–) has been U.S. Senator from Massachusetts since 1962. He ran unsuccessfully for president in 1980. He was divorced from his wife, Joan Bennett, in 1981.

Kara (1960–)
Edward Jr. (1961–)
Patrick (1967–)

Kara Kennedy

Kara Anne Kennedy, the first of three children of Joan Bennett and Edward M. Kennedy, was born on February 27, 1960, one year after her father had passed the Massachusetts bar examination. She grew up in a much-publicized family—the world knew about the problems of her father and mother, and her brother Ted Jr.'s cancer.

After Edward Kennedy was elected to the U.S. Senate in 1962, the family moved to Washington. Kara attended National Cathedral School for Girls. Her classmates from Cathedral remember Kara as shy but exceptionally pretty, and a kind and sympathetic friend.

Like her Kennedy cousins, Kara was exposed to competitive sports, politics, power and public service at an early age. Also like them, she had to cope with great sorrow. Her Uncle Jack was assassinated when she was three, and her Uncle Bob was shot five years later. When Kara was thirteen, her twelve-year-old brother Ted had his right leg amputated. Kara was a constant presence, cheering him up and helping with his recovery. She also helped take care of her youngest brother, Patrick, during recurring asthma attacks.

At the same time that thousands across the country poured out their love and sympathy for Ted, Kara carried a private sorrow: her mother had become an alcoholic. Joan Kennedy's husband and children loved her and tried to help her overcome her disease, but it was many years before she was able to begin the slow process of recovery. Kara helped persuade her mother to join Alcoholics Anonymous and frequently attended meetings with her. After her father's 1980 campaign for president, he and Kara's mother were divorced. A family friend notes that, "To this day, the devotion of Kara, Ted Jr. and Patrick to each other and to their parents is exceptional." Senator Kennedy, despite the divorce, still demonstrates regard for Joan by sending her flowers on her birthday and at Christmas.

Although Kara had been deeply troubled by the crises in her family, her father was a staunch ally. She graduated from National Cathedral in 1978 and enrolled at Tufts University. During her college years she had contemplated a career in international relations, but while working on her father's 1980 presidential campaign, she developed an interest in working with the media.

After finishing at Tufts in 1983, Kara joined the staff at Metromedia Television in New York City and became an associate producer. In 1988, when her father was again campaigning for the Senate, she moved to Boston where she and Ted Jr. were co-campaign managers of the reelection team. She coordinated media relations and traveled throughout the state speaking on her father's behalf. After the election, Kara became part of the documentary crew at Channel 4, the NBC affiliate in Boston.

In September 1990, Kara was married to Michael Allen, a Washington, D.C., architect. The wedding was on Cape Cod, at the same church where Caroline Kennedy was married to Edwin Schlossberg. The reception was at the Kennedy compound at Hyannis Port. The Allens live in Washington, D.C.

Edward M. Kennedy Jr.
The Earliest Victor

Adolescence is awful at best. It's the time when children fall apart—emotionally, socially and spiritually—so that later they can put themselves back together as adults. And right smack in the midst of adolescence is age twelve.

When young Teddy Kennedy was diagnosed as having cancer at age twelve, that certainly wasn't his only problem. Although he was a child of a wealthy, prestigious clan, none of that wealth or prestige, nor its legendary intelligence, influence, or energy, could help Teddy. He had to fight his cancer alone.

A small lump was discovered in Teddy's leg after he hurt it playing football. A bruised and swollen area below his right knee throbbed and hurt for a very long time. Though his pediatrician recommended applying warm packs to the injury, it didn't help.

Doctors at Georgetown University Hospital diagnosed the problem as chondrosarcoma, a rapidly growing cancer of the cartilage. That was in November 1973.

Joan Kennedy, Teddy's mother, was just coming to terms with the grim realization she was increasingly dependent on alcohol and had entered a treatment center in Switzerland. She was called home with the news that her first-born son was in the hospital and quite sick. By the time she arrived back in Washington, the diagnosis was complete. The malignancy was particularly virulent. Amputation above the knee was recommended as soon as possible.

If a limb has to be amputated, surgeons desperately try to save the joint if at all possible. With the leg, the knee joint provides mobility and flexibility for walking and running; it also facilitates the fit and application of the prosthesis. The amputation of young Teddy's leg above the knee joint indicated the seriousness of his cancer.

Teddy's dad, Senator Edward Kennedy, was doing his best to serve as stand-in father for his slain brothers' children, all thirteen of them. Ironically, his niece Kathleen, Robert's oldest daughter, was scheduled to marry David Townsend the very day of young Teddy's surgery. Reflecting the clan's concern, the couple offered to postpone their long-planned wedding, but they were encouraged to go ahead despite their cousin's ordeal.

Once the decision had been made by the doctors, Ted had a talk with his son the night before the surgery. It was more difficult than any of his hundreds of political speeches or public statements. Later, he mused, "The brain can only take so much, and the heart can only stand so much. I'd never have forgiven myself if I had handled it badly."

Gently, Ted broke the tragic news to Teddy, sat with him awhile, then left to attend Kathleen's wedding rehearsal, where he was the surrogate father about to give away the bride.

The next morning, Teddy's father was at Georgetown University Hospital as the operation began. After doctors assured him there were no complications, Ted headed for Holy Trinity Church, a few blocks away. Father James English, assistant pastor of the Kennedys' parish, Holy Trinity, was at the hospital during the early morning surgery and then followed the senator to the church to perform the wedding ceremony. English recalls, "With that amazing Kennedy style, you'd never have known there was anything wrong. The bride was radiant. The groomsmen all wore top hats, which all somehow disappeared. Rose was lovely. It was a large and magnificent wedding and there was a huge crowd of well-wishers outside of the church." As the male leader of the family, Ted was determined to show that in the midst of sadness there can be joy, and the family could gain strength from both.

Skipping the wedding reception, Ted hurried back to the hospital to be at his son's side in the recovery room. English was there, too, and recalled: "Teddy was a perfect little boy. It was impossible to believe he was without his leg. They brought him into the room and as the boy was still under the sedative, his father leaned down and put his forehead close to his son's chest. The boy instinctively put his arms around his father's head, and he just held on, and held on, and held on. It was the most beautiful moment I've ever witnessed."

As brutal as the surgery was, it was only the beginning of a long, painful, and frightening ordeal for the twelve-year-old. Doctors gave him one chance in four of survival.

The Kennedy clan rallied, as usual. Cousins and aunts and uncles came by to cheer Teddy up and give him support. The nation responded to yet another Kennedy tragedy with an outpouring of tears, letters, gifts, and prayers. But it was up to Teddy to bear the pain.

Stunned by the diagnosis and suddenness of the operation, hospital staff did the best they could to maintain professional decorum amid a daily parade of Kennedys and their notable friends. Nurses, aides, and doctors would linger in the halls for celebrity spotting and a chance opportunity to meet the famous.

After the surgery, Teddy's work began—he had to learn to walk all over again. Daily physical therapy sessions at Georgetown University Hospital were exacting to the point of being tough, and almost cruel, to such a little kid.

"Stand up straight," demanded the therapists. "You can do better than that. Come on, one more time." They knew their job was to give this disabled young man the determination and new skills he would need to live a normal life.

But still, he was only a boy. His parents stayed with him as much as possible. Aware that the cancer could show up in another part of his body, his mother was tempted to treat him like a fragile treasure.

But from the outset, Teddy would not allow any such pampering. English visited just after Teddy came home from the hospital. "I expected him to be in bed and was amazed to find him clomping up and down the steps and the hallway, racing around with the other kids. He insisted on showing me his stump and his new leg and how it all worked."

Ted and Joan gave their son a high-powered telescope which he kept on a terrace outside his bedroom. After the long and difficult days of treatment, Teddy and his mother spent evenings together studying the constellations. The wonder of the universe and its vast, beautiful complexity gave a perspective to their great struggle and lent a sense of peace to the troubled mother and her determined son.

The terror of Teddy's illness also gave Joan new strength. Her son needed her. Since the birth of their first child, Kara, Ted had insisted on having help—baby nurse, cook, nanny, secretary, and housekeepers. But after Teddy's traumatic operation, he depended on his mother for the emotional support he needed. He was brave for the doctors and therapists, and tough with his cousins and friends, but with his mother he could let down and cry. She drew from her inner resources, without the help of alcohol, to give her son what he needed.

Cancer is a frightening disease. The invidious way its cells attack and grow, avoiding detection and changing to overcome proven treatments, make even the most informed cancer specialists wary and respectful.

Teddy's age made controlling the disease even more tricky. It's not unusual during adolescence for a youngster to grow six or eight inches during a year. The puberty growth spurt and increased hormonal activity could have caused the cancer to crop up in other places in the young man's body, such as in his cartilage or in any of his vital organs.

Understandably, the family sought the most aggressive treatment possible. Using his influence as chairman of the Senate health subcommittee, Ted scoured the country for a program to save his son.

Dr. Emil Frei of the Dana-Farber Cancer Institute in Boston headed an experimental chemotherapy program that used methotrexate. His preliminary studies showed some hope for malignancies like Teddy's. The treatment was rigorous and extremely uncomfortable, involving intravenous injections of the chemical every three weeks for two years. Teddy had to be hospitalized four days every three weeks for the duration of the treatment.

Either Ted or Joan was always with Teddy on these four-day weekends, flying to Boston on Thursday, checking in to Children's Hospital, and flying back to Washington Monday morning. The treatments were as uncomfortable as Dr. Frei had described, so Teddy's parents spent the nights in his room to help him through the nausea and pain. The methotrexate was administered in huge doses intravenously for six hours. Its effects are poisoning, and an antidote drug called a citrovorum factor was administered every five hours for the next three days to flush the methotrexate from his system. His dad learned to inject the antidote so he could get Teddy out of the hospital a day or two early and continue the treatment at home.

The first two nights of treatment were the worst. Often by the third day, on Saturday, Teddy would be ready to have cousins or friends come to the hospital to keep him company. Two of his best friends were his cousins, Joe Gargan Jr., and John Kennedy Jr. The boys were within three years in age, with Teddy in the middle, and had spent summers romping together in Hyannis Port. All three were named for their fathers and the Children's Hospital nurses dubbed them "The Three Musketeers, Junior." When Teddy was up for rough-house or mischief, his cousins responded heartily and often spent the night with him at the hospital.

Thus it went for two long years. Every three weeks, Teddy endured the chemotherapy treatment, pain, vomiting and hair loss, followed by tests and X-rays to check the results and see if the cancer was spreading. The biggest worry was that the cells would attack Teddy's lungs, so chest X-rays were performed regularly. Even the relief that a treatment session was over, was tempered by the fear that the X-rays would reveal metastasis, the spread of the disease.

Teddy and Joan struggled together to deal with their respective handicaps, cancer and alcoholism. Through difficult times, their relationship strengthened. In the midst of the chemotherapy ordeal, Teddy once told his mother, "Mom, you're doing fine, too. If you don't go back to your drinking, I won't go back to my cancer."

Joan countered by telling him he was luckier. "Five years and you're in the clear, Teddy. I have to give up alcohol for life."

Teddy answered, "Yeah, Mom, but you get to keep both legs."

Skiing with One Leg

Life-threatening circumstances often force a child to deal with his own mortality, and bring an unusual maturity and depth. The long-term, critical, invasive nature of Teddy's illness gave the adolescent a new view of priorities.

Within the first year after Teddy's surgery, Father English got a call from a fellow Jesuit, Father Gene Linahan, chaplain at the National Institutes of Health. He had a patient much like Teddy, a young man who had been a champion swimmer at his school, whose leg had also been amputated because of chondrosarcoma. "I got permission from the senator, and from Joan, and picked up Teddy at St. Alban's after school," said English. He took Teddy to meet the other youngster. "The boy's mother and I pretended to be talking but we were watching the boys. They were like two little old ladies talking about their operation. Teddy told it just like it was. That was probably the beginning of his career of reassuring and talking to children with cancer."

Kennedy kids pretty much have a ticket to do whatever they want with their lives. Some of them, at times, are seen as self-centered and destructive. The temptation to take advantage of the Kennedy power can be great. Young Teddy's brush with mortality gave him an early appreciation of his good fortune.

In talking about his chemotherapy treatments, Teddy said, "I felt like I just wanted to run away and never go back to the hospital. My initial thought was, 'I don't care. I'm just not going to do this anymore. Why don't they just leave me to die?'

"When I went into the hospital for my cancer treatments, I'd see the same kids in there who had been there during my last visit. I'd go back just for a few days every three weeks, yet they'd be in there for months and months. I began to feel sort of lucky that I was as healthy as I was."

With this attitude, and bolstered by the celebrated Kennedy competitiveness, Teddy pulled himself out of the doldrums. Four months after the amputation, Teddy was on the ski slopes with the rest of the family.

He soon discovered skiing with one leg is not easy. In 1974 very few handicapped people even attempted to try such difficult sports. Regardless, with two legs or one, Teddy was determined to keep up with his family and to make it seem as natural as possible. The sight of a one-legged kid coming down the mountain on one ski with a small ski attached to each of his poles for balance was odd but inspiring.

Teddy's attitude about the loss of his leg has made it easier for other people to deal with it. From the beginning, he unabashedly used the word *cancer* and insisted on showing his stump to family and friends. That type of grit motivated the others to give him equal treatment and not favor him as being disadvantaged.

In work, as in play, he asked—and received—no favor. His governess required him to do his chores as soon as he was able. "Teddy, it's your turn now and don't complain. When I was your age I had to milk twelve cows before I did anything else in the day. Get on with it."

The cousins took the same attitude in family touch football games at Hyannis Port in Massachusetts and the Hickory Hill estate in McLean, Virginia. Teddy recalled, "They never allowed me to feel like I was different. If there was a football game being organized, they'd always say, 'C'mon out.' And my cousins threw the football to me just as hard as they would to anybody else. I'd look 'em in the eye as they were coming in and I'd say, 'Oh, aren't you big coming in and roughing up some poor little kid with one leg!' "

Teddy's strength in dealing with his handicap has helped sensitize and inform the American public of the needs of the disabled. Because he is a Kennedy, pictures of him bellyflopping on a sled with his dad or skiing on one leg down a mountain have circulated worldwide in the press and given power to other people to go beyond their disabilities. Pictures of Ted Kennedy Jr. walking along in shorts, with his prosthesis in full view, have eased the self-consciousness of others with artificial limbs.

Teddy's natural appeal and upbeat outlook have helped survivors of cancer as much as the handicapped. Surviving cancer is an often unrecognized aspect of the disease. The diagnosis and treatment are harrowing and all-absorbing. But once that crisis is over and the patient is alive and well again, survival requires a total change of focus. No longer is there an immediate concern with illness or the threat of death. The survivor must get on with the present and future.

In Teddy's case, the damage of cancer is always there as a reminder—he has an artificial leg. He can't run well. He walks with a slightly uneven gait. But he doesn't want to be recognized as a cancer patient. He is a cancer survivor who is living life to the fullest.

He feels a responsibility to reassure and to prove to others who are suffering from cancer and disability that life does go on indeed. He has visited cancer units around the world and talked with patients, especially children, explaining just what happened to him, answering questions about his prosthesis, his recovery, and his family. He shows them how the leg works, demonstrating the knee joint and how the prosthesis attaches to his stump. "It's like sticking your finger in a coke bottle. The suction holds it on." He often tells them that things will be hard for them—that their recovery will get more and more difficult. But his example is reassuring— here's a young person who survived and is leading a wonderfully normal life.

Teddy Kennedy finished St. Alban's School in Washington, D.C., in 1979, and graduated from Wesleyan University in Middletown, Connecticut, in 1984 with a degree in American Studies.

For his twenty-first birthday, in September 1982, his sister Kara organized a weekend party on Nantucket Island for about twenty family members and friends. Tops among the toasts was younger brother Patrick's: "You might say Teddy is a great partier . . . and it's true. And you might say Teddy is a great lover . . . and it's true. And you might say Teddy is a brave guy . . .

and it's true. But I know something better than any of you. He's the greatest brother that ever was."

After finishing college, Teddy became an ardent advocate for the civil rights of people with physical and mental challenges. His focus is to address the problems of "handicappism"—the systematic exclusion of individuals with disabilities and the myths that are perpetuated by this segregation—in many different ways.

He started a nonprofit advocacy group, based in Boston, called Facing the Challenge. It represents those he calls the "physically challenged" on issues concerned with housing, transportation, accessibility, job discrimination, parental leave and insurance coverage. In Teddy's view, "The real handicap we face is not the one of accident or birth, but the one created by society. The sooner we remove the physical barriers to equality, the sooner the more stifling attitudinal barriers will fall."

Teddy set aside his work with Facing the Challenge to manage his father's 1988 campaign for reelection to a sixth term in the U.S. Senate. He and his sister, Kara, co-managed a campaign that returned their father to the Senate with his largest margin ever. While building the campaign organization, Teddy made contacts around the state. Political speculators assume this Kennedy will some day use these contacts for his own candidacy. Perhaps—but that's not his immediate agenda.

His father privately urged him to run for the lieutenant governor's post in Massachusetts, but Teddy said no. For now he has set aside the political platform. No more speeches, no more testifying before political policymakers, and fewer visits to hospital cancer wards. Facing the Challenge is no longer active, though Teddy's interest in the handicapped is still strong. He taught a course on disability policy at the John F. Kennedy School of Government at Harvard University in 1989. He is a member of the board of the Hole in the Wall Gang, a summer camp Paul Newman sponsors for children with cancer, and through constant correspondence, he encourages cancer victims in their fight for survival.

Ted Kennedy Jr. doesn't shy from the public limelight, but he is taking time to assess and develop his interests before deciding which direction to take. He is an active board member of Very Special Arts and Special Olympics International, charities run by his cousins, and he serves on the President's Committee on Employment of People with Disabilities.

Currently, Ted lives in New Haven, Connecticut, where he is pursuing a graduate degree in environmental affairs at the Yale University School of Forestry and Environmental Studies. Environmental and ecological issues are areas of passionate interest. He is a competitive sailor like his dad, and finds the challenge of serious sailing and the peaceful commune with the sea as a way to refresh his spirit.

A warm, gregarious man, Ted combines his father's strength and self-confidence with his mother's sensitivity. He naturally reaches out to support needy people as well as other causes. He is committed to educate the American public on issues affecting the physically challenged, and to teach by example as well as by advocacy that all are entitled to the same basic treatment and rights—and to compete for opportunities—regardless of physical or mental abilities.

Patrick Kennedy
Footsteps

The phone rang in the office of Jack Skeffington, the longtime state representative from the 9th Rhode Island district. It was his old friend Joe DeAngelis, speaker of the Rhode Island House.

"Say Jack, I've got some information for you. Patrick Kennedy's running against you."

"Who's he?" asked Skeffington.

"He's Teddy Kennedy's son, and he lives in your district."

"Should I be worried?"

"Let me put it this way. I wouldn't want him running against me."

Mount Pleasant, Elmhurst, and Olneyville are the neighborhoods of the 9th District. People go to work, gather in church, give birth to babies, and bury their dead there. Many elderly, on fixed incomes, struggle at a subsistence level. The majority of the middle class, the retired, and those about to be, live a life without glitter. And consider it more or less good.

It's not a place accustomed to life-size legacies. At least, not until Patrick began to call West Providence his home. The youngest of Edward and Joan Kennedy's three children says, "I belong here. I've got roots."

He plans to stay awhile, because on September 15, 1988, while still a sophomore at Providence College, the people of the 9th chose Patrick for state representative.

How did it happen? "I campaigned my tail off," says the soft-spoken Patrick. "I went door-to-door and enjoyed it. It was competitive. I'm competitive. It was a race. And I won."

The engaging, brown-haired Kennedy's summerlong

172

effort unseated Skeffington, a 49-year-old funeral home director who had been representing his home district for the past ten years. Four months after his triumph, Patrick recited the oath of office, placing his left hand on the same bible his Uncle Jack had used, on January 20, 1961.

Using that bible was Patrick's idea. He had often seen it during visits to the John F. Kennedy Library, where Dave Powers is curator. On New Year's Day, Patrick pulled the late president's close friend away from a football game, extracting his promise to get the bible down to Providence.

Of course, it was a good prop. But Patrick's reasons went deeper. A successful political campaign would be an important rite of passage for any young man, and he was the youngest Kennedy ever to hold elective office— a nice distinction in a very distinctive family. The bible helped connect Patrick to his legendary uncle—the nation's youngest president.

Using his own two feet, Patrick was now part of more than just a small state legislature—he was following in familiar family footsteps. He said:

> I probably nipped in the bud that nervous anxiety that would always have been with me. You grow up in the family I've grown up in and try to figure how you fit into it. Of course, you're identified by that legacy of your uncles. You wonder what it would be like to get involved in politics. I'm sure I would have always had this nagging question, wondering whether I had it.

Wealth, power, ambition, courage, religion, self-sacrifice: the low road mixed with the high. Patrick emerged out of a complex family culture, learning with the taste of his mother's milk and the feel of his father's ambition, that merely to be born, to live, and to die is not enough.

> That's what my grandmother always said. She quoted the old proverb: "To those who have been given a lot, much is expected." That was something I was aware of growing up. I think more than anything else, you wouldn't feel like you could live a fulfilling life unless you could measure up to being able to give back.

To be sure, Patrick had received a lot. Yet a series of family tragedies caused Patrick's childhood to be less than idyllic. Chronic attacks of asthma put him repeatedly in the hospital. Cancer claimed his brother Teddy's leg. Three uncles were shot down. His father broke his back in a plane crash. His mother sought refuge in alcohol and pills from a life grown too full of stress. His parents struggled with their relationship. A cousin overdosed on drugs. And right before his first political campaign, he had to deal with a life-threatening tumor:

> I was forced to grow up pretty quickly. I'm not uncomfortable to say, I don't have a full sense yet of who I am, what my needs are, and what I'm all about. But I'm finding out. It's an exploring kind of period; and happily, an enjoyable one.

Six years before Patrick was born, Uncle Jack and Aunt Jackie moved into 1600 Pennsylvania Avenue and redecorated the nation with Kennedy vigor, style and youth. A bullet pierced through the veneer of Camelot. Yet the legacy passed to Bobby. Ten months after Patrick was born, Bobby, too, was slain, leaving only Ted.

As the years went by, the late president's children— Caroline and John—had to learn a way of fitting into the larger-than-life legacy. Nothing on their birth certificates or in their trust funds guaranteed success. Patrick explains what it's like to be part of the next generation of Kennedys:

> You either act on it or react to it. It's an either/or decision. You either like it and move in that direction or if you don't, it's because you don't like it and you're going to run away from it and do something very different. In either case it's going to shape what you are.

Catching the Political Bug

"When I first got to know Patrick, he didn't think he wanted to get involved in politics," said Jim Vallee, Patrick's roommate at Providence College. "But then he kind of caught the bug, and now it's mainly what he talks about. He loves it."

While finishing up at Phillips Andover Academy in Massachusetts, Patrick decided to go to college close to home in Virginia. But before the end of his first week at Georgetown, he realized he had made a mistake.

"I was living on campus, but my home in McLean, Virginia, was right there, too," he explains. "I couldn't distinguish my own identity. Everyone I would meet and all the contacts I would make were through people who knew my father."

Patrick decided to go to Rhode Island. Providence was close enough to family; it was not Massachusetts; it was Catholic; and he could make it his own.

Upon meeting with Dr. Raymond L. Sickinger, his faculty adviser, Patrick asked, "Is there an agency where I can volunteer to do some work for the needy?" Sickinger gave Patrick the number of the St. Vincent de Paul Society in downtown Providence, and Patrick volunteered a day or so a week.

On campus, students and professors came to know him as an engaging kid who demanded a lot of himself.

An open smile and respectful attitude charmed neighbors on his block. Patrick eschewed behavior and unseemly parties often associated with youth.

Courses in political science, religion, American studies, and history attracted him most. With a full schedule on and off campus, he put just enough time into his studies to get Cs and Bs—and an occasional D.

While working at a summer job at the Rhode Island Public Interest Research Group (RI-PIRG) Patrick decided to run for delegate, which meant taking a quick step out of neighborhood anonymity. It took some people by surprise when they learned just whose Patrick this was. Next-door neighbors Angelo and Dora Mendillo remembered, "Patrick was living here on Sharon Street for months and we didn't know it. One day Mr. Solomon, his landlord, said, 'Do you know who's living on the first floor? It's Patrick Kennedy. But don't tell anyone.' "

His barber agreed. "I was cutting this kid's hair for two years. But I never knew he was Patrick Kennedy until I opened the paper one day and saw his picture."

The lanky young Kennedy was elected president of the Providence College Young Democrats. Then he and John Tabello, executive director at RI-PIRG, worked out a deal. Patrick wanted to be a delegate to the Democratic National Convention; Tabello wanted to strike out on his own as a political consultant. So a new company, Impact Rhode Island, was born. Patrick was its first client. He won a delegate seat and headed to Atlanta, where his idea for his more famous cousin John to introduce his father was both a family and convention success.

Back in Providence, Patrick sized up his opponent. In 1986, Skeffington had lost 48% of the vote to a 22-year-old challenger. Roommate Vallee encouraged his friend. Patrick's father sensed his eagerness. The family talked it over. The waters seemed inviting. Should he go for full immersion?

"I tried to point out the advantages and disadvantages," his father recalled. "The race was his decision. Patrick is very much his own man. He had fire in his belly."

Patrick and Tabello mapped out a campaign strategy, and then linked up with Chris Nocera, an energetic young political activist Patrick had met in the Rhode Island Young Democrats. Nocera had been laboring in party trenches ever since his junior high school days. People in the 9th knew Chris—either from his political work, his liquor store, or church. They liked him. But when State Democratic Committee members failed to appoint Nocera to a position he thought he had earned, they left him a still loyal—but wounded—Democrat.

Another Bad Back

Before Patrick could decide whether to run, he had to deal with a strange, unexplained pain in his back. It had been bothering him for several months, and tests were inconclusive.

One night the pain grew unbearable. A friend took him to the emergency room of Rhode Island Hospital, but doctors there couldn't detect the cause. So he went up to Massachusetts General Hospital. They did a Magnetic Resonance imaging test—and found nothing. He promptly returned to Providence and lost all feeling in his legs. "My whole balance was off," says Patrick. "I was bumping into things."

He returned for another MRI. This time they found a tumor at the base of his neck. They hadn't seen it earlier because they were looking at his back and legs, where the pain was the most acute. The tumor was growing larger each day and threatening his spinal cord. They couldn't wait. The next morning, hospital orderlies wheeled him into the operating room. Fourteen hours later, after a delicate operation, the tumor was successfully removed.

The doctors said later that the way the tumor was growing, in another week it might have cut the spinal cord off and paralyzed him for life.

Patrick came home to a party for him in the neighborhood, organized by Nocera and hosted by his neighbors, the Mendillos. The doctors had told him to take it real easy; he still had not declared. After about three hours he went home and called his close friend. "Jim," he said, "it's a go. Would you come down for the summer and help?"

In a neck brace, and newly aware of the preciousness of life, Patrick started walking the district.

"We walked every night together," says Vallee. "He never complained about his back. The doctors said it was a miracle that he could come back the way he did after the operation."

"We did a poll to make sure people were open to Patrick," said Tabello. "They were. Then we designed one of the most sophisticated get-out-the-vote efforts you'll find anywhere. We had megapeople working eighteen-hour days on the campaign."

Patrick began walking the district. He and his team lined up supporters. George Hoey, a feisty, salt-of-the-earth activist and an undertaker like Skeffington, at first kept at arm's length from the Kennedy campaign. He had buried a lot of people from the 9th and 10th districts from his funeral home located across the street from Blessed Sacrament Church, where Patrick still attends Mass and teaches catechism classes on Monday night.

Patrick's campaign staff finally arranged for Hoey to meet with their candidate. Like Nocera, Hoey was carrying a grudge against party regulars. More than thirty years earlier, before Rhode Island adopted signature identification at the polling stations, he had lost a race for the school board by a few votes in an election he was convinced was rigged.

Hoey thought vaguely that some day he might want to run again. Then along came Patrick. Hoey liked him from the moment they met. Through Patrick, he would get his revenge. Besides, as a business competitor, he could neutralize Skeffington's advantage. When there was a death in the district, Skeffington would hurry out a personal condolence card with an implicit message: "Who better to bury the dead than your friendly, concerned representative?" A Skeffington defeat would be good for Hoey's business.

Residents encouraged Patrick. They said they never saw Skeffington and barely knew who he was. Patrick did not hesitate:

> I saw this as a terrific opportunity to carry on the torch, as they say. We have a chance to take it, OK? And then if we take it we can light places with it. Hopefully I can light up a little bit of Rhode Island.

Skeffington was not just any representative. He was a party insider with a decade of receiving and dispensing favors under his belt. To party leaders, he was loyal, dependable, and well-liked. He was one of them. They resented this Kennedy kid from PC—this rich carpet-bagger. When Patrick called on the party bosses, they closed ranks around their own. "Be patient," they told this new kid on the block. "Wait your turn. Pay your dues. Lick envelopes. Run errands. In time, we'll call your name."

Although he did not get their support, Patrick was not disheartened, for he knew that they didn't control how the people in his district would vote. Except for one state senator—Dave Cruise, formerly a staff member for Patrick's father—no prominent Rhode Island Democratic leader broke ranks. After his election victory, Patrick reflected on the machine politics of Providence:

I faced a situation where I wanted to run for public office, and I was told to wait my turn. This was totally repugnant to me and I fought that. It turned out I had to fight the whole Democratic Party to win.

Politics is boss in Rhode Island. Nothing much happens without it. Patrick's three-year-old roots in the neighborhood were small cache to a party machine that enforced the discipline of waiting your turn.

"The state representative is a local office," says Patrick. "It is personal. People want to feel comfortable with their rep."

The small districts of 10,000 or so people are about the size of two parishes. Patrick planned to visit every house, attend every meeting, and respond to every call. Once he won, he would owe the party bosses no favors. Over time, he could mend broken fences.

"Because they were calling me an outsider, it was all the more important that I go and meet the people. The people, not the party leaders, are going to give their endorsement," Patrick declared. "I'm taking my message directly to the people door-to-door."

Patrick planned to outhustle Skeffington. He knew he could outspend him. He was determined to outsmart him. He did all three, and he won.

"They had computers," Skeffington complained, nearly a year after his defeat. "And all summer long, Kennedys came in. They would divide everything up and go walk the neighborhood. They even visited my ex-wife four times. I could run against Patrick. But running against the entire family was tough."

Skeffington raised money, spent money, worked hard and shed twenty pounds in the summer heat. But Patrick, his organization, his family, his funds and his friends, were too much.

Patrick walked the district throughout the hot summer. House-to-house. Knock, knock, knock. Face-to-face, with sparkling eyes and a charming smile. "Hi, I'm Patrick Kennedy."

Wherever he knocked, he considered it his vote to win; where he missed, he considered it Skeffington's. It was hard work, and he loved it.

When they polled ahead of him, it would go 55 to 45 for Skeffington. After a knock on the door, it came in 60 to 40 for Patrick. People would pour out their hearts to Patrick of what his uncles had meant to them. To see this Kennedy kid in the sweltering heat, top button fastened, tie pulled up, impressed the locals. They filled him with food and drink and covered him with hugs and kisses.

Damn those Polaroids

"I don't hold a grudge," said Skeffington. "Winning and losing is what politics is all about. But damn those Polaroids. It hit the news at 10 a.m., and people started coming in all the way from Warwick, to get their pictures taken around a bunch of Kennedys. I tell you, if it had rained, we would have won."

Patrick's father had dropped in during the summer. In general, the campaign considered it an asset for the Kennedy cousins to participate. They reasoned that voters were comfortable with Patrick's younger contemporaries, but they were concerned that voters might feel intimidated by the famous father. Even more to the point, Patrick needed this to be his victory, both in reality and in perception.

I did not want "the Senator" to come in. When he did come, which was twice, I wanted him there as my father. I was concerned not to play into the fears of people. This was Patrick running for representative, and Patrick who would personally represent them, not "the Kennedys." That is why I even debated whether he should come in on election day.

"We're trying to develop Patrick here," Hoey would say.

After working the polling places beginning at 7 a.m. on the day of the Democratic primary, Ted's back was sore. He has never fully recovered from when he broke his back in a private plane crash in 1964. Though visibly in pain, Ted went to Hoey's garage and started calling people to get out and vote for his son.

"Hi. I'm Ted Kennedy. I want to urge you to vote for my son, Patrick. . . ."

It didn't hurt.

Patrick's older sister, Kara, and his older brother, Teddy Jr., spent time in the 9th district. They would hook up with one of the locals and go knocking. Having lost a leg to cancer when he was 12, Teddy Jr. was hauling his thirty-pound prosthetic around the neighborhood. It got tiring. He would start to look for houses without steps. Sometimes he would go out with Hoey, who subjected him to his own brand of humor:

"Hi, Betty. This is Teddy Kennedy Jr. He's Patrick's brother," Hoey would say at a door. "You know Patrick's running for state rep., don't you? Well, Teddy wants to tell you about what Patrick's going to do for the district.

"Would we like some iced tea? Sure," said Hoey. "And by the way, have you got some WD40 for the leg?"

Patrick arranged for his father to appear at a campaign picnic in Coventry, south of Providence. Hoey put Patrick to work grilling hot dogs and hamburgers ("but I can't cook," protested the candidate) and then went out to meet the father-senator, who was flying in nearby. Hoey waited. And groused. And waited. The senator finally came, an hour late. As Hoey sped to the picnic, driving much too fast, he seized this precious opportunity where he, George Hoey, by virtue of his privileged position with Patrick, could chew Ted Kennedy out. An animated Hoey recalls the ride, and conversation: "What do you mean," I said to him, "telling me to slow down? You're the one who was an hour late. And just keep your damn Massachusetts opinions to yourself. You keep the hell out of Rhode Island politics. Patrick's the first Kennedy in Rhode Island. Let him develop it."

"Teddy had ideas on procedures, on what we should do in the campaign," explained Hoey. "I told him, 'I don't have to listen to this nonsense. We're not coming on like gangbusters around here. This kid has humility; he has a lot of character. He's got an opportunity. Now, screw off.' "

According to Hoey, "Ted was astounded. Nobody ever talks back to him. I chewed his ass off. I said, 'You don't mean anything to me.' "

The Kennedy campaign plowed through the summer. During the final week of the campaign, fresh volunteers from Providence College reinforced the regulars. By election day, the campaign's twenty to twenty-five volunteers had swelled to over a hundred. The PC students did a mail drop to every house in the district at 5:00 a.m. on Election Day morning. The day proved a triumph of organization. Each worker tracked thirty potential Kennedy voters, firmed them up for Patrick, and offered a ride to the polls. Computer printouts listed names of known supporters who had not yet voted. They were called. The campaign used two-way radios, hand-counted voters, and knew exactly what was going on from when the polls opened at 7 a.m. until they closed.

While working the crowd at Mount Pleasant High

School, Patrick quipped, "I want to dispel the rumor that there are more Kennedys than voters in the 9th district today."

U.S. Representative Joe Kennedy—eldest son of Robert and Ethel—started it off at the Nathanael Greene School. He posed for pictures, helped old ladies up the steps, and down the steps, and gave away hugs and kisses.

When Joe's shift ended, John Kennedy took his place. The family worked throughout the day, covering all seven polling locations. A much larger-than-usual voter turnout provided the margin of victory. In 1986, 1,624 people voted. Skeffington spent $9,000 and won by 106 votes, 880 to 774. The Kennedy-Skeffington race pulled in 2,333 out of 4,779 eligible voters. Patrick won by 1324 to 1009—57 to 43 percent.

The Rhode Island legislature is a part-time job, in session about 60 days a year and paying $5 a day. During the campaign, when asked the size of his budget, Patrick said, "Whatever it takes to get my message across. I am responsible to do everything possible to win."

According to Nocera, it took $114,000, or $86.40 a vote, making it the most expensive state legislative race in Rhode Island history. Patrick personally contributed $14,000, and pulled the rest from family sources, running up a $100,000 debt.

Representative Kennedy

Patrick often overcame opposition or skepticism with his personal and political graces. However, he could not have overthrown an established political base without some people getting upset.

"Patrick Kennedy hurt a lot of people," says Ellen DeGeorge, a Skeffington supporter and staff member in the office of House Majority Leader Christopher Boyle. "He will learn that people have long memories."

Dan Sweeney voted for Skeffington. "It seems there's getting to be four parties in this country," he says. "Democrats, Republicans, Independents, and Kennedys. I have no need for the Kennedys in Rhode Island."

Nino Silvestri has a two-chair barber shop on Chalkstone Avenue a block from the Skeffington Funeral Home. Skeffington is a longtime customer. "I work two jobs, ten hours a day. I don't have much use for someone who never has to work a day in his life. Frankly, I was surprised he won. People didn't care too much for him coming in here and spending so much money. And you know what else? I resent a dynasty. We still want everyone to have an equal chance to be president."

Elmer Cornwell runs a different kind of shop. A Brown University professor of political science, he specializes in Rhode Island politics and closely observed the 9th District race. "If someone walks in from out-of-state with a fat bankroll and moves in, it is not viewed with enthusiasm," he says. "But once he won, the leadership accepted him. It's the old adage, 'If you can't beat 'em, join 'em.'"

As State rep., Patrick has blossomed. This child of exceptional privilege found adoption as West Providence's favorite son.

"People come in from out-of-town and ask, 'Is this where Patrick Kennedy beat the undertaker? How'd he do it?' I tell them all the same thing: 'Once you meet Patrick, you'll know.'" Ilene DiMaio of Smith's Restaurant is a great Patrick booster. "He doesn't expect any favors. He waits his turn for a table. I told his father, 'We're keeping him fed, and looking after him.'"

Once in the General Assembly, Patrick watched and listened, feeling his way around. He asked for the Health, Education and Welfare committee, and got it. He brought out a major piece of legislation, on something he feels strongly about: gun control.

Opponents told Patrick that nothing could be done to stop the NRA. "But we shouldn't acquiesce," he replied. "A sense of defeatism won't get us anywhere."

His father wants a federal ban on handguns. Patrick's approach was politically realistic for Rhode Island. While doing his homework on the issue, he found statistics to show that criminals don't only buy guns on the black market. Many are purchased from legitimate dealers, so a longer waiting period allowing for an adequate background check would be sensible.

With fellow representatives Rene Menard and Linda Kushner, Patrick brought out legislation calling for a ban on a wide range of guns and a longer period for background checks. He learned through Kushner that after Maryland passed a bill requiring a waiting period before someone could purchase a gun over the counter, 782 applicants were screened out.

"Not too many people could challenge my credibility on this issue," said Patrick. "No one can lecture to my family about the danger irresponsible people can do with guns."

Patrick was pleased at the end of his first legislative session in late June 1989. In an arena where freshman representatives are to be seen and not heard, Patrick sponsored and got passed a voter registration bill to facilitate citizen participation in the electoral process. His bill calls for the state government to actively register voters, by offering voter registration at state offices and services such as the Department of Motor Vehicles. The occasion of registering a car or getting a license is now an opportunity to register to vote.

Hoey maintains that Patrick was as green as could be when he first came knocking. If so, he quickly ripened. Unified opposition to him ended on Election Day; peace with the party leaders quickly followed. A *Journal-Bulletin* headline on March 29 read: "Patrick Kennedy is now one of the 'ins.'"

Patrick opened a small office at 1000 Smith Street. A three-story Victorian frame house converted to law offices sits midway between his home and the Providence College campus, just two miles from the State House. A sign out front says, "Patrick Kennedy, Representative." Two Noceras staff his office: Chris as his paid administrative assistant; Chris' wife, Erin, as a regular volunteer.

As a Kennedy, Patrick's load is heavier than that of most other state representatives. Twenty to thirty letters come in each day, about one-tenth of them from outside the state. It may be someone asking for help to get a street light put in so elderly people can walk to the grocery store. Or a request for a piece of his legacy: "My grandmother is in a nursing home. A note from you would perk her up."

A note came in from Walnut Creek, California: "I am approaching my 75th birthday. Some 29 years ago I voted for your uncle, John, for president of the United States. If you hurry, I may be able to vote for you, as well, for president."

After the first several months of observing the comings and goings of the new representative from her perch as receptionist at the Smith Street office, Evelyn Simone told him: "Patrick, you're young. You're working so hard, and missing out on so much."

"No I'm not," he responded. "I love what I'm doing."

Simone thinks Patrick is amazing for his age. "He's very much in demand. They love him in the district. He's unique. He really is."

After a summer of campaigning and his first legislative session, Patrick the politician began hitting his stride; developing technique. The son of perhaps the best orator in the Democratic Party is intent on becoming a good speaker himself. He accepted speaking requests when he could, especially from groups of young people. By the end of his second legislative term, in the summer of 1990, Patrick had even ventured out of state for a successful fund-raising speech for a political candidate in Maryland:

Now history for me is starting to come to life. We can be part of our own lives. We don't have to always relive something we don't know anything about from personal experience. As far as my uncles are concerned, I was born in 1967.

I had a sense growing up with a father like my father who was always working on the unfinished business of President Kennedy and Attorney General Robert Kennedy. I also saw what my Aunt Eunice, and all my aunts, had done with the Special Olympics and other projects. I saw all the things my family was working on. I saw my cousins beginning to do things.

It's a very powerful legacy. I know that just through the response people have given me. Going door-to-door I can't hear enough about my uncles, my father, what they've done, and what my family has done. That imposes some obligation to continue.

Father and Son

"No question about it. I would have liked more time with my father when I was growing up," says Patrick. "But I was close to my father, always accepted by him, no matter what age I was. Now our relationship is exciting."

Ted was a proud father when Patrick chose to run. He urged his son and his organization onward, throughout the campaign. Thrilled by Patrick's victory, he exclaimed, "None of *my* political victories have meant as much to me as this."

Families customarily gather together for funerals and weddings. The Kennedys routinely gather for political celebrations as well. In the family tradition, they didn't let Patrick down. With his father, mother, cousins, and friends surrounding him at an election-night victory celebration at Caruso's Restaurant, Patrick looked over at his cousin, Douglas. A college junior across town at Brown University, Douglas was living amid the fanfare of Patrick's political emergence.

"You would think he might have felt a little jealous," says Patrick. "But he wasn't. He was beaming at my success. I'll never forget that, as long as I live."

There's nothing quite like the relationship you have with your family. It's not based upon what they can get from you, what you can get from them, and those sorts of things. I grew up with my family, rather than my peer group.

Part of family life for Patrick had been traveling with his father and sharing the frenetic pace and disappointment of the 1980 run for the presidential nomination. He experienced national politics "not as a fairy tale; it's not Camelot—it consists of real live people getting things done without a lot of grandeur and pomp."

Patrick has been with his parents at their peaks; he has also seen them in their valleys. Sometimes they were able to be there for his needs. At other times they weren't. When Patrick was a child, his father learned to give him injections to help him breathe during severe asthma attacks. Patrick once gave him a poster with a large caricature of a nurse holding a platter with a huge syringe. He inscribed it, "To Dad, my night nurse. Love, Patrick."

Patrick has learned much about human strength and frailty during the first twenty-three years of his life. His experiences and spirituality lead him to observe, "By an accident of fate, I am related to some people who have made an enormous impact in the direction this country has moved."

A couple of years prior to his first political campaign, Patrick's father arranged for a rare few days of private time with the younger of his two sons at a Catholic retreat house.

It was just my father and me. We had a chance to get some personal guidance from the retreat master, a Jesuit priest who spent eighteen years in India and has captured the powerfulness of Eastern spirituality. He emphasizes the importance of a coming closer to God. You can see your life as God's pattern, see ups and downs as different trials God has put you through.

While Patrick has launched himself in one direction, there are some people in the wings who believe he's missing a truer calling. A picture in his office is inscribed by Boston archbishop Bernard Cardinal Law: "To Patrick Kennedy: Wishing you God's abundant blessing, and hoping that you will keep your options open."

Father Charles Maher, Patrick's pastor at Blessed Sacrament Church in Providence, agreed. "I am disappointed he hasn't yet decided on the priesthood. He's the one for it, but I'm working on him. He's going to the seminary."

It's Patrick's custom to say the rosary to his 100-year-old grandmother, Rose Fitzgerald Kennedy, when he visits. Her hearing is nearly gone, so Patrick needs to speak loudly. He introduced Jim Vallee to her, intoning: "Grandma, this is my friend from Providence. We go to Catholic school together. We say prayers before class." Grandma's face lit up.

He's serious about God. But "Patrick a priest!" exclaims Hoey. "No way. He's no priest. Not with Kathleen O'Brien. Have you seen her? She's really great, and wonderful with kids. I think the future might be P.K. & K.O."

Patrick explains that he and his close friend of a few years "have a relationship that we've allowed to grow. It's serious, fulfilling, and long-term."

What Next?

Working locally, establishing roots and making contacts, and running successfully for a second term in September 1990, Patrick dismisses the question about where he may go from here. State representatives tend to serve two or three terms before burning out or moving on. After two terms, at age 25, Patrick would be eligible to run for one of Rhode Island's two congressional seats.

"I expect him to run as soon as he's 25, in 1992," says M. Charles Bakst, political columnist for the *Providence Journal-Bulletin*. "He could go for either the First or Second Congressional District—whichever would be easier. That family is not too particular about residency."

Rhode Island is a small state—and he is a Kennedy—but moving from its General Assembly to Congress would still be a large jump. Most people would need to serve in a visible statewide office in between.

Patrick believes in a Democratic Party "in the tradition of FDR," one that asserts government's major role in making a positive difference in people's lives. He views such a tradition as distinct from a Republican Party that wants government to stay out.

Patrick thinks the Democratic Party has taken a bad rap as being protectors of the weak. During his first campaign, he was challenged by a homeless, smoking, alcoholic with a heart problem to declare what he would do for the homeless. Patrick retorted: "I see you're smoking. What for? That won't help your heart. How's society going to help people who are not going to help themselves?"

"There's a real problem in defining ourselves as a party," he comments. "The first priority is to make opportunities available for people, and to move away from the idea that we're a welfare state. That's a terrible image."

At 23 years of age, the two-term state representative is still several credits away from a college degree. Yet out in his district and down in the State Capitol, Patrick is building for a future of people needing him to be someone larger than life. Patrick the politician must not only continue to get the stoplights put in; he is a Kennedy, and many people will also want him to minister to their spirit. He has not stepped back. He is moving in a direction which will enable people to vest him with their hopes and fears. He is exercising his instinct that it is more blessed to give than it is to take.

Patrick attracts certain adjectives to himself like metal filings to a magnet. He is "nice, respectful, sincere, caring, deep, kind, hard-working, soft-spoken." He is also analytical, purposeful, focused—and feeling. College friends think he is "neat—a really great guy."

In Patrick's small living room, books lie in piles all over—Elie Wiesel's *Night* and William Manchester's *Churchill* are recent books that he has read. He enjoys a meal of chicken marsàla with corn, mashed potatoes, and bread. It cost $6.95, a take-out order from Smith's. He drinks some orange juice he picked up at the local convenience store.

Patrick likes attention. He likes the pleasure of a political challenge and the power to be able to do good. Does he mean to stir dreams in hearts he has touched; does he connect to people's unuttered hopes?

Where he will go is not up to Patrick. He can only decide how far he will reach—and why. At the beginning of the twenty-first century, a 33-year-old Patrick will have had ten more years of developing and maturing, in a nation redefining itself in a dramatically changing world.

Will Patrick continue in the world of politics and try to make a difference? Vallee sees a world of possibilities for his friend. Powers does, too. "Jack said he found politics more rewarding than any other profession. It challenged him to use all his faculties. Patrick sees it as Jack did," he says.

Sailor Jack Fallon also likes what he knows of Patrick's valor and courage. Patrick once whipped off his shirt and jumped in the ocean water after the old wooden boom crutch fell off his father's sailboat. About twenty people on the boat began clapping for Patrick, who had seized the opportunity to be a hero.

Another time a sailing accident put a life at stake. Though too old to captain the America's Cup, Fallon was still rugged. While sailing with the Kennedys three miles from shore, a swinging boom knocked him into the water. The day was windy. The waves were high. Patrick saw that the fast-moving boat was leaving Fallon behind, so he jumped into the water with a life preserver. When he got to Fallon, he discovered the old skipper had been knocked unconscious. Patrick kept him afloat until the boat could come about and pull them out of the water to safety.

"Believe me, Patrick's a chip off the old block," says Powers. "He's just like Jack. Jack was truly committed to a belief in the nobility of public service. So is Patrick."

Ted Kennedy has explained that all Kennedys try to steer away from a comparison with Jack or Bobby Kennedy. "Many people ask, 'How are you going to follow in their footsteps?'" says Patrick. "I can't. They are different people than I am. I have to do what I'm able to do and in the best possible way."

Friends of Patrick, talking among themselves, say they hope he stays clean.

"He won't get corrupted," says Hoey. "He's too solid."

"I think he has the best shot of all the Kennedys," says Vallee. "He appeals to people more than any other. I think most people see it that way."

"He revitalized the entire neighborhood." And Leonelli's wife adds, "Patrick is deep beyond his years."

The eyes of the elderly beseech him with hopeful glance: "Patrick, do good for the nation. Can you heal us? Can you deliver us? Please don't betray us." They allow him gently to poke at the embers of ancient hopes. "No one ever bothered with us before," says an elderly neighbor. "He made all of us feel like we mattered."

Old men and old women listening for footsteps, daring again to dream dreams. Will young men and women have visions? Time will tell. Time will tell, how large his political parish.

Footsteps. Footsteps. Where will they lead?

Epilogue to the Paperback Edition

Two folders lie on my desk. One folder says "Kennedys." The other folder says "Kennedys."

Inside the first folder are articles, clippings, and interview notes on the nearly-royal Kennedys, the first family of American politics. Open the folder and discover stories of public service, tales of idealism, leadership, caring, courage, success, grace, wit and humility.

The second folder also contains articles, clippings, and interview notes, but on a different Kennedy family. These Kennedys appear to be America's most publicly dysfunctional family. This folder reveals stories about infidelity, sexual promiscuity, alcoholism, drug abuse, decadence, aimlessness, arrogance and hubris.

Which folder reveals the true Kennedys? Both, to a degree, and neither. However, in the past eighteen months since the publication of the hardcover edition of *Kennedys: The Next Generation*, the second folder has become the fatter. Yet with less fanfare, the public service folder keeps filling up as well.

The Kennedy cousins inherited a mixed tradition in which idealism and opportunity for leadership compete with the trappings of an elite lifestyle as the wealthy members of America's only political family dynasty. When this heritage mingles with the extraordinary public curiosity about their private lives, the result is a volatile mix.

Whether in pursuit of political office or entangled in yet another Kennedy "lifestyle" episode, Kennedys have the capacity to explode into public attention. Which is just what happened after the event of March 30, 1991, when William Kennedy Smith was accused by thirty-year-old Patricia Bowman of rape. William instantly leapt from undistinguished anonymity as "the quiet one," and the only Kennedy to choose medicine as his career, into an incident that became the biggest liability to the family name since Uncle Ted drove off the bridge at Chappaquiddick.

Any minor Kennedy-related event becomes an item in the newspaper. The rumor of a run for political office generates priceless publicity, whereas a good Kennedy scandal becomes a national obsession. Lest any of the twenty-eight living Kennedy cousins needed a reminder of what it means to be who they are, William awakened them in a manner they and their families will never forget.

With William's rape trial as the centerpiece, 1991 was not a good Kennedy year. The televised gavel-to-gavel proceedings brought a view of Kennedy lifestyle into American homes that was a long, long way from "Ask not what your country can do for you . . ." and "From those to whom much is given. . . .".

The year also seared Ted anew into the national consciousness, but not because of his advocacy of national health insurance or some other legislative program. Instead, the extent to which his excessive drinking and antics are influencing the young of the next generation became the national "topic." The senator is facing a re-election race in the fall of 1992 and it seems that for the first time since dinosaurs roamed the earth, he may not be returned to the Senate by automatic voter decree. He will likely adorn his campaign with his thirty-eight-year-old fiancée and Washington, D.C. attorney Victoria Reggie at his side, hopefully suggestive to the voters of stability and family values.

The Year of the Trial also saw the bloom of Camelot fall further off the rose with the publication of a book by historian Thomas Reeves, in which JFK's already legendary sexual forays are depicted as jeopardizing national security. In *A Question of Character,* Reeves also reveals that, by the way, Kennedy didn't actually write his Pulitzer prize-winning book *Profiles in Courage.*

And there was more. In his new biography of Peter Lawford, author James Spada writes of Bobby Kennedy leaving Ethel and the household of kids back home while he satisfies himself with Marilyn Monroe, including a covered-up appearance with the troubled actress the day of her mysterious death. In Milton, Massachusetts, Ted Kennedy's ex-wife Joan was arrested for drunken driving, once again, and ordered to undergo rehabilitation. About the same time, with a newly-earned master's degree from the Yale School of Forestry and Environmental Studies in his hand, Ted and Joan's eldest child, Teddy, Jr., signed himself into the Institute of Living in Hartford, Connecticut, to deal with his admitted alcohol problem.

He explained, in a written statement:

> At times, life has presented me with some difficult challenges and I am doing my best to face up to them. Recently I have taken an important positive step in my life. I have spent the last three weeks in an alcohol treatment program. My decision to seek help was based on my belief that continued use of alcohol is impairing my ability to achieve the goals I care about. I hope that others will respect my right to keep my personal life private.

Younger son Patrick, a Rhode Island state representative, had already sullied the portrait of legislative accomplishments in Rhode Island with images of late night bar-hopping with Dad at Au Bar. Then came a revelation in the *National Enquirer* that six years earlier Patrick, too, was among the considerable ranks of cousins who had a serious encounter with drugs. While a senior at Phillips Academy in Andover, Massachusetts, he had checked himself into a New Hampshire drug rehabilitation center during spring break.

In response, Patrick sent every constituent in his district a letter assuring them his prep school drug problem would not affect his work as a state lawmaker. "While I believe the problems of my adolescence have no bearing on my public service, the dramatic increase in sensationalized publicity surrounding my family has led to their public disclosure," the letter said. "I love my family very much. We have been through a lot together, and we will continue to support each other. If sensational news accounts about me and my family have been the price of public service, then the confidence you have placed in me to serve you has been the reward. Because of you, the reward far outweighs the price."

He released a statement in the *Providence Journal* which said: "As a teenager I started down the wrong path in dealing with the pressures of growing up. I mistakenly believed that experimenting with drugs and alcohol would alleviate them. I have taken no drugs whatsoever since then and I use alcohol only in moderation."

One cousin came publicly to his defense, in an interview for the *Boston Globe.* Patrick is "a practical politician and at the same time an utter idealist," said Bobby Kennedy, Jr. "He's like my father, who was uncomfortable being the center of attention. He doesn't deserve what's happened to him in the last two weeks. It's the exact antithesis of who he is."

"Now I see what this last name means, the kind of attention it can bring," said Patrick a few days after the events of the Easter weekend. "This week I learned the down side of public life."

Down in Florida, following Patricia Bowman's accusation and the subsequent lodging of criminal charges against William, and as the Kennedy public relations and legal apparatus moved from the bridge of Chappaquiddick to the sands of West Palm Beach, it was not at all certain whether the family could control the tide. The possibility remained throughout the spring and summer and into December that the image of a Kennedy facing down Khrushchev and of young American idealists working out of Peace Corps huts would have to make room for a newly crafted portrait, this one of a Kennedy—even if his name is Smith—as convicted rapist adjusting to a less tony lifestyle behind the bars of a Dade County, Florida prison.

But it didn't happen. The prosecution's case was weak. The Kennedy damage-control machine did its job in the specifics of William's defense, and the medical school graduate was acquitted. In the end, the jurors applied their common sense. The incidence of a single woman who gets picked up at a bar and goes back to the Kennedy estate with a single man carries with it an implicit sense of having something other than mutually discussing the historical context of Jack Kennedy's American University speech in mind.

The Kennedys breathed an enormous and collective sigh of relief. Writing for *Vanity Fair,* Dominick Dunne described William's thank-you speech outside the courthouse following the jury's decision: "His beaming family looked on proudly, as if he had won an election rather than an acquittal."

Which, of course, he had. Not his but theirs. Or at least, he had escaped the ignominy of being the Kennedy cousin who had most screwed everything up for the others. After all, it wasn't *his* political fortunes he had put at risk. He was becoming a doctor. Sure, his defense reportedly cost $1 million, with a good chunk coming out of his own inheritance. (He is reported as saying he has to borrow money to pay the bills.) And he may find women less willing to strike up a casual acquaintance. But his life was to be private. The Kennedys who are choosing public and political pursuits and whose lives express a dedication to uplifting the family name and the *virtues* attached to their legacy would be the ones most bruised by William's debris.

For nine months, the media and public consciousness sculpted his twenty-seven cousins into the sordid environment of the trial with William in the forefront and them in relief. In addition to Patrick and Ted, who both were called to testify, nineteen family members came into the courtroom. Among William's aunts and uncles, only Jacqueline Kennedy Onassis chose not to appear.

Many cousins also put in appearances, including John Kennedy, Jr. The trial showed that despite obvious internal family stresses, when the stakes are great, the Kennedy family still pulls together. The cousins inherited the family name and tend to exhibit a collective sense of responsibility to maintain it. They know their destinies are intertwined.

Before, during and after William's trashy tabloid scandal, the other cousins continue to get on with their lives. While William skulked off to the University of New Mexico in Albuquerque and began 1992 by starting his residency in internal medicine, many of his cousins continued to fill up the first folder, the one about Kennedy idealism, accomplishment and public service.

Caroline Kennedy Schlossberg was one of those leading the way. She completed a serious book with co-author Ellen Alderman and they were out together on a book tour during the spring of '91. The terms set for talk-show hosts and journalists seemed to be, "Interviews on the book, yes. Personal questions, no." Of course, being who she is, she could dictate the terms and maintain the decorum of her carefully guarded privacy. Questions about cousin William were unthinkable.

In Our Defense: The Bill of Rights in Action illustrates each of the first ten amendments to the Constitution. Her book was well-reviewed, and with the publicity power of the daughter of the former President, became a national bestseller and provided a forum through which Caroline could express herself publicly on a topic of passionate interest.

Caroline said in an interview with Susan Linfield for *McCall's* magazine, "The Bill of Rights has worked, for two hundred years, to protect the individual against the power of the government. People should be proud of it. It gives us all the opportunity—and the responsibility—to create the kind of government that's close to our hearts."

Now and then a few personal questions were sneaked in. Caroline has been admitted to the New York Bar but says she does not envision practicing law in the near future because "My kids are too small." The president of the Kennedy Library Foundation adds, "But I learned a lot from doing the book, and my partner and I are talking about writing another. It would have to be an idea I'm really excited about, though, because I love being with my kids."

Caroline's brother, John, continues in his career as an assistant district attorney in Manhattan and with his un-official designation as America's (the world's?) most eligible bachelor. At the same time William's defense was being prepared in Florida, John was developing his skills as a prosecutor and tried his first case in August. The jury returned a conviction in the week-long burglary trial. "Winning is better than losing," said the young assistant D.A.

With John becoming established in his career and Caroline standing on the foundation of her book and public appearances, America's former first children felt it time to come out a bit more in the public, with an extensive interview appearance on "Prime Time Live" in May 1992.

For a long time, the Kennedys have sought to shift public attention away from the deaths of Jack and Bobby to what they accomplished while alive. In 1988,

Kerry Kennedy Cuomo founded and became executive director of the Robert F. Kennedy Center for Human Rights. One activity is to present human rights awards on or about November 20, her father's birthday.

John F. Kennedy's children followed suit. Two years ago the family created the Profiles in Courage Award, to honor politicians who place principle above politics. The 1992 award was presented on the seventy-fifth anniversary of JFK's birth and provided the occasion for Caroline and John to appear for a taped interview on "Prime Time Live."

In the interview, John said of his father, "He would have wanted us to go on with our lives and not reenact his."

But what of following in his father's footsteps? John said: "My father was a politician, my uncles were politicians, my cousins . . . . The answer is a big, 'I don't know yet.' When I do, you'll probably find out.

"You have to remember," he said, "both Caroline and I—particularly me—view my father's administration through the perception of others, through photographs, and what we've read."

Had he seen Oliver Stone's movie, *JFK*?

"No. Let's not forget the subject matter. It's not entertainment for me. It's not a subject which I've spent a great deal of time analyzing."

Regarding what happened in Dallas, "Whatever they decide or find will not change one fundamental fact—that it's not going to bring him back."

Caroline said that she thought her father's greatest legacy was "the way he inspired so many people and especially young people to get involved in politics and public service."

Is that torch still lit?, Caroline was asked. "I think it's up to all of us to ensure that it still is," she replied.

Shortly afterward, in late May, the Capitol Hill rumor mill in Washington, D.C. was humming with talk that

John Kennedy, Jr. might run for elected office, right now, and go after the Manhattan congressional seat held by Manhattan U.S. Rep. Ted Weiss.

"Totally groundless," said a Kennedy spokesman. But suggestive.

Whether or not . . . or when . . . John comes to know that he wants to enter politics, cousins Michael Kennedy and Kathleen Kennedy Townsend have no doubt. For Michael the time was nearly now. The head of Citizens Energy Corporation in Boston was seriously considering running for the 11th Congressional District seat being vacated by Rep. Brian Donnelly. Though Michael lives just out of the district, in Cohasset, candidates do not legally have to live in a district to run. However, sources close to the family say that with Ted concerned about a potentially tough race for re-election and with Joe running for re-election from the 8th Congressional District, the family decided it would be unwise to have three Kennedys on the ballot in the same state at the same time.

For Kathleen, her unsuccessful 1986 campaign in Maryland for Congress is well behind her. A fourth daughter—Kerry Sophia Kennedy Townsend—born on November 29, 1991, the lack of an available race, and a satisfying job that she has crafted out of the State of Maryland's requirement that public schools offer credit to kids who work in their communities, all will keep her put for now. "I think what I'm doing is very worthwhile," she says; but, "Yeah, I'd run again."

In November, 1991, Anthony Shriver presided over "A Night of the Stars," a charity ball for about fifteen hundred guests at the Departmental Auditorium in Washington, D.C. to benefit Best Buddies.

Anthony explained that he has been devoting seven days a week for the past four years to the program he founded, which connects college students to persons with mild to moderate mental retardation. Today, by all accounts, Best Buddies is a major success. It has six offices and oversees forty-five hundred participants in one hundred eleven collegiate chapters nationwide. Anthony spends most of his time on the road, opening thirty to forty Best Buddies chapters a year and with a goal to start one on every college campus in the country.

Six weeks before William's acquittal, Anthony said about Best Buddies, "These are the kinds of things my family is interested in, what we spend ninety-nine percent of our time on." The scandal has "absolutely not affected what I'm doing. I just go out, stick to it and push ahead. Maybe one day people will pay attention to that instead of what's going on in Palm Beach.

"I don't spend all my time running around Florida, Aspen or Europe chasing girls," he said. "I work to *enhance* the reputation of my family."

Nor does Maria Shriver run around chasing men. The star of NBC's "First Person with Maria Shriver" and husband Arnold Schwarzenegger gave birth to their second child, another daughter, on July 23, 1991. While Maria was at the hospital, Arnold came to see her and their newborn in his newly-acquired, $45,000 Humvee all-terrain vehicle. You know, just like the ones used by U.S. troops in Operation Desert Storm, which he customized by having "Terminator" painted on both sides and installing a cellular phone, black leather seats imported from Austria, and an elaborate stereo system.

A member of the Kennedy clan by marriage, Schwarzenegger said to Sally Ogle Davis in an interview in *Redbook*, "Why is the entire family always categorized as 'the Kennedys?' There are Lawfords and Smiths and Shrivers and many other families besides the Kennedys. It is a very happy family. They are very helpful in every respect so I am delighted to have them as family and friends."

And he is helpful too, in particular with an occasional behind-the-scenes boost to his cousin-in-law, Christopher Lawford, who by his account finally emerged a few years ago from almost twenty years of drug use and is now pursuing an acting career and gradually building a list of screen credits. "I never intended for drugs to wreck my life," Christopher told *People* magazine, "but that's exactly what happened. They threw me up against the wall and said, 'We got you now, son.' Thank God it's over."

Christopher Lawford is thirty-seven years old. His cousin Joseph Kennedy II, at age forty the oldest among the male cousins, will soon vie for his fourth term as congressman from Uncle Jack's old district. On May 19, 1992, Joe stood up on the floor of the U.S. House of Representatives and denounced the broadcasting of his uncle JFK's autopsy photographs on national television. He said that he and his eleven-year-old twin sons were stunned to see the gory photographs while watching "NBC Nightly News."

"I want the people of this chamber to know how outrageous an act I feel that was, how harmful to my family I feel that was," he said. "We ask for one thing, which is that the autopsy photographs remain private. And last night the national news [NBC] chose to break that request."

Meanwhile, a few months earlier in the print media, while cousin William was on trial, Joe was featured in *The Washington Times* riding his bike along the C&O canal in Washington, D.C. He is a dedicated fitness cyclist and has introduced legislation that would require states to set aside three percent of federal highway money for construction of bike paths and pedestrian walkways.

"More than ten million bikes are sold in this country every year," he says, "and it's time to put them to use for transportation, not just recreation." He advocates state and federal governments working together and investing in creating safe conditions for cyclists and pedestrians.

For another cousin, Bobby Shriver III, 1991 was a year to leave his venture capital investments work behind, head west to Los Angeles, and take over the direction of Special Olympics Productions. This summer, along with other cousins, he'll take a couple of days off for the wedding of his brother, Mark.

The three youngest children of Bobby and Ethel Kennedy have been moving their lives along. Max Kennedy was married on July 13, 1991 to Victoria Strauss, the daughter of the chairman of the Pep Boys auto supply and repair chain. Awhile after his 1990 graduation from Brown University, Douglas Kennedy took a job as a general assignment reporter for the *Beacon*, a weekly newspaper in Nantucket. Rory Kennedy has been working in Washington, making a documentary film with Robin Smith on crack mothers and their babies.

On Election Day in November, in Massachusetts and Rhode Island, with Ted, Joe, and Patrick on the ballot, Kennedys once again will ask the American people for the privilege of representing them, of providing leadership. They will have William's trial just one year behind them.

Though the Kennedy name was tainted, they are a family well-tempered by adversity. They draw on a reservoir of strength that includes the energy and money and emotions that it has taken for campaigns and service in Congress, the Senate, and the presidency, as well as innumerable public service projects, significant wealth, two assassinations and constant public exposure for over forty years.

Whether the goal is an acquittal or an election, the Kennedys know how to rally. They did it for William and they'll do it again. As the cousins continue to mature and advance, a Kennedy running for national office will again serve as the spark for the American people's collective emotions.

The cousins are no longer about the "next" generation of Kennedys. They aren't about the past. The cousins, finally, are about their own lives, a reality that neither desire, nor achievement, but only the passing of time could grant.

Jonathan Slevin
June 1992

Index

About the Authors

Jonathan Day Slevin is a journalist, writer, and editor based in northern Virginia and a principal in the literary agency of Slevin, Cooper and Spagnolo. His most recent book is *Black on Red: My 44 Years in the Soviet Union* co-authored with Robert Robinson. In addition to writing part of this book Mr. Slevin, with Maureen Spagnolo, were the principal editors. He wrote "Patrick Kennedy: Footsteps" and the short sketch on Rory Kennedy.

Maureen Spagnolo is an uprooted Brit who now lives in the Washington, D.C. area. She has worked as a staff writer for *The Washington Times* for several years and as an editor for a Washington-based magazine, *The World and I.* She wrote "Kathleen Kennedy Townsend: A Winner Who Lost."

Tom Andersen has been covering the environment for Gannett newspapers since 1985, and lives in New Canaan, Connecticut. He wrote, "Robert F. Kennedy Jr.: White Knight of the Environmental Crusade."

Jeanne Viner Bell is a Washington, D.C. based public relations counselor and writer. She is president of the American News Women's Foundation. Her work has appeared in books, magazines, and professional journals. She wrote: "David Kennedy: The Lost Son," "Kerry Kennedy: It's the Cause that Counts" and many shorter sketches.

Mary Gorman is a feature writer for *The Catholic Standard*, the *Journal* newspapers, *Forcast Magazine*, and the American Podiatric Medical Association. She wrote, "Teddy Kennedy Jr.: The Earliest Victor."

Michael Gross is a contributing editor and columnist for *New York* magazine. He is the author of seven books, including biographies and mystery novels, and is a former columnist for the *New York Times*. He has written cover stories on celebrities for such magazines as *Vanity Fair, Manhattan, Inc.* and *Saturday Review*. He wrote, "John Kennedy Jr.: Disgustingly Normal."

Paul Keegan, whose work has appeared in *Mother Jones, Travel & Leisure* and *New England Monthly*, is senior writer for *Boston Business Magazine*. He wrote, "Michael Kennedy: One to Watch."

Adria Hilburn Manary is a freelance writer living in Annandale, Virginia. She has worked as director of development of the New York Special Olympics. She wrote, "Joe Kennedy II: Heir Apparent," "Robert Sargent Shriver III: The Shriver Balance," and also contributed to the piece on Kathleen Kennedy Townsend.

Susan Price is a freelance writer based in Los Angeles. She wrote, "Maria Shriver: The News Breaker."

Annette Tapert is the author of three books on military history. Her most recent book, co-authored with Nancy Lady Keith, is *Slim: Memoirs of a Rich and Imperfect Life*. Ms. Tapert wrote "Caroline Kennedy Schlossberg: A Very Private Person."